TEXTILES NOW

DRUSILLA COLE

Published in 2008 by
Laurence King Publishing Ltd
361-373 City Road
London EC1V 1LR
email: enquiries@laurenceking.co.uk
www.laurenceking.co.uk

A catalogue record for this book is
available from the British Library.

ISBN: 978-1-85669-572-5

Words and image selection:
Drusilla Cole

Cover illustration: 'Black Tree'
© Ilkka Timonen for Virtuelli
Design Studio

Project editor: Gaynor Sermon
Copyeditor: Carol Franklin

Book design: Rudd Studio
www.ruddstudio.com

Printed in China

Author's dedication

I would like to dedicate this book to my
lovely daughters, Emily and Peggy, for
their constant love and support.

Acknowledgements

The author and publisher would like
to thank all of the contributing artists,
illustrators and designers for their time,
effort and generosity of spirit.

TEXTILES NOW

DRUSILLA COLE

LAURENCE KING PUBLISHING

CONTENTS

INTRODUCTION

Textiles Now contains a wide selection of my personal choices of mostly three-dimensional contemporary textile designs; they range from the awesome to the amusing, and all have inspired me in one way or another. These designs have been sourced from artists and designers from all around the world who have been gracious enough to send their work for inclusion in this book. The featured textiles have been produced using a wide range of traditional and experimental techniques, and I have included those that particularly excite me in their use of colour, pattern or texture, or in their emphasis on exploring technical boundaries.

Many of the designs exaggerate or otherwise distort scale to produce dramatic effects; several are inspired by the flora and fauna of particular regions; many pieces are concerned with issues of sustainability and use natural dyes, recycled fibres or eco-friendly methods in their production, which is doubtless a growing theme. In particular, hand dyeing using natural plant dyes is making a comeback in areas as diverse as North Wales, Australia, the US and Japan. The return of the soft yet rich colours of plant dyes such as madder, woad and weld is once again exerting an influence on many areas of fashion and interior decoration, and is becoming more widely used in place of the ubiquitous ranges of chemical dyestuffs and colourants.

I believe that some of the most innovative textile designs are those that employ deliberately haphazard or random techniques to create unique and utterly beguiling artworks. The techniques themselves are often not necessarily new, but the methods of compiling or combining them are. In this age of rapid actualization of images and ideas, it frequently appears to be the case that true innovation is accidental. It is testimony to the skill and courage of the designers and artists that they are able to recognize and respond to such developments in order to create such appealing artwork.

I requested that the contributors provide me with background information about their designs – their inspirations, methods of working, and choice of materials – and their words provide an extraordinary insight into the creative minds of the artists. Wherever possible I have included quotes from the artists along with the descriptions of their work; as well as a priceless record of their intimate thought processes, these words offer a unique understanding of their specialist craft practices.

The book is organized into three main sections according to the predominant techniques used to create the textile designs. Within these sections I have broadly arranged the entries by colour, which I hope adds to its charm and creates a delightful visual rhythm. This was one of the most enjoyable tasks of what has proven to be a very intense and fulfilling project.

Drusilla Cole

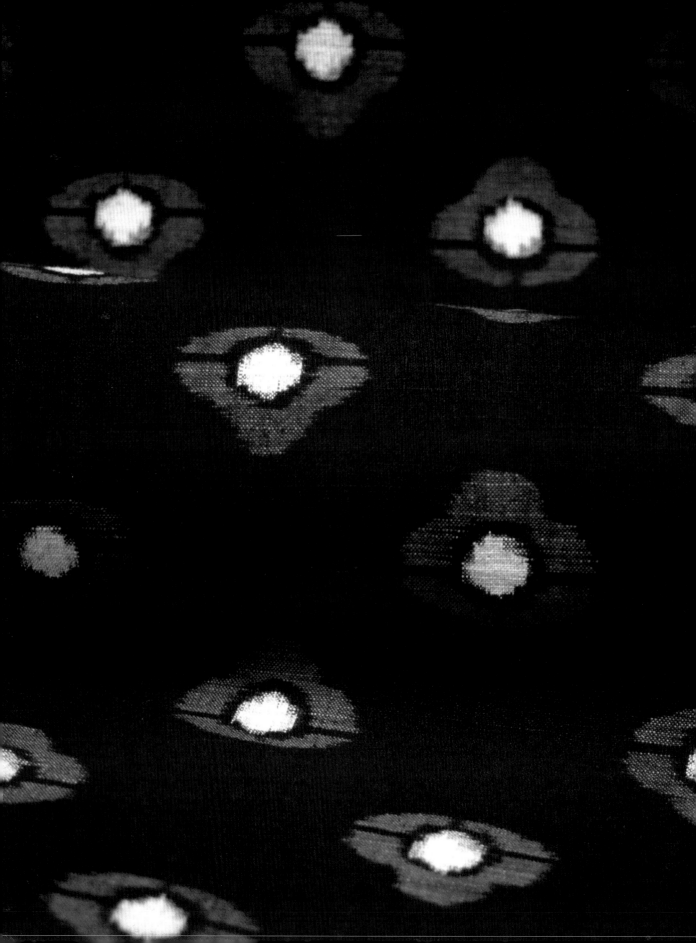

CONSTRUCTED

This first section features three-dimensional textiles that use primarily natural fibres, yarns and fabrics to create garments, tapestries, lengths of material, decorative items and art installations. These beautiful, highly tactile pieces achieve their surface decoration by means of manipulating their component parts. Also included are innovative pieces of textile art by artists who use stones, wire or beads in their work to form patterns that challenge the idea of textiles being constructed exclusively from fibres.

For all textile artists the use of colour is fundamental, but the examples featured in this section demonstrate that the quality of texture – whether experienced or perceived – can be the most important part of the design. The artists accomplish this by utilizing a range of highly skilled traditional and experimental techniques, from felting and folding to knotting and pleating.

Many of these pieces have been hand dyed prior to their use, with some artists even growing the natural dyes they use themselves. Several examples use hand felted fabrics, and a number feature fabric folded into pleats and sculpted into three-dimensional shapes. Where appropriate, textiles are shown in context to demonstrate their end use, such as garments created from the artists' own woven, knitted, felted or crocheted fabrics, or used in accessories and soft furnishings. However, it is the intention of many of the textile designs to be purely and simply thought-provoking works of art.

Christine White 'Glacier Bay' 80 x 15 cm (31 x 6 in). The artist comments: 'Ironically, it was while working to create a felt that would mimic the dark-coloured mud crack pattern seen on a dried-up lake bed when this pure white, ice-like piece emerged. I work in white on white when I wish to sharpen my focus on structural line and in this case the texture emerged pure, strong and simple. Even the way it moves evokes floating ice packs in a cold, glacial sea.' The unique texture was created by using a laminated felt technique, bonding white merino wool onto sheer silk and manipulating the bond at certain points in the feltmaking process.

Jessica Preston 'Monochrome Circles' 50 x 38 x 6.5 cm (19.5 x 15 x 2.5 in). Hand dyed and manipulated into three-dimensional forms, these striking black-and-white layered cotton fabric pieces are intended for use in interiors, as fashion accessories and in commercial and public displays.

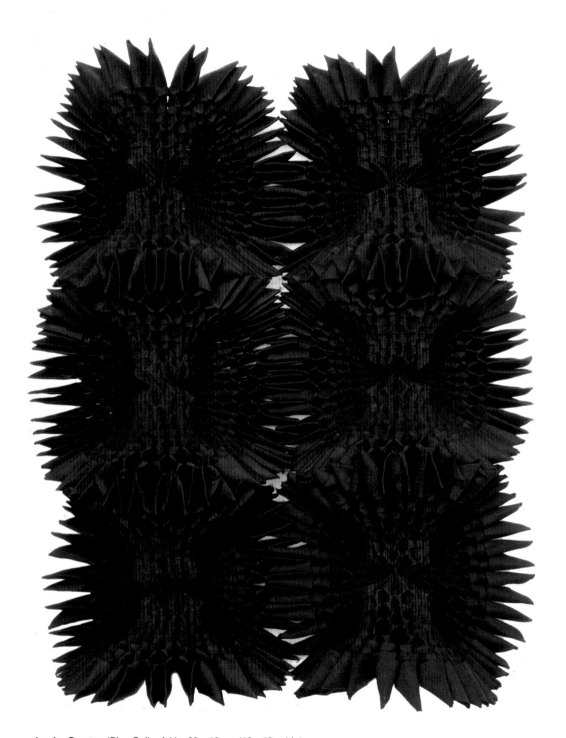

Jessica Preston 'Blue Spikes' 41 x 33 x 10 cm (16 x 13 x 4 in).
Pleated, folded and manipulated into delicate peaks, this hand
dyed monochromatic cotton structure is a striking example of the
artist's approach to textile art.

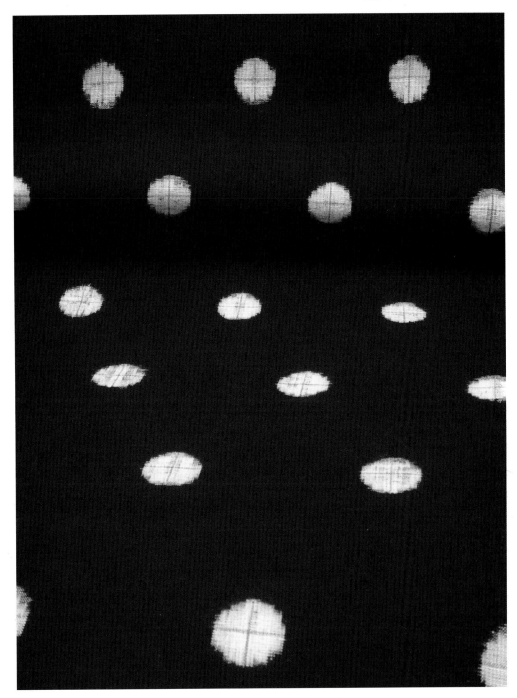

Chinami Ricketts 'Crossed Dots Kimono Yardage' 38 x 1370 cm (15 in x 45 ft). Drawing on historical kimono patterns, this artist uses both hand and machine spun cotton, which she binds, dyes with indigo and weaves entirely by hand on an antique Japanese loom built specially for *kasuri* (ikat) weaving. Working this way, the artist takes about two months to complete one length of kimono cloth.

Deanne Fitzpatrick 'All You'll See is the Back of Me'
107 x 97 cm (42 x 38 in). This artist draws inspiration from her childhood spent in a coastal village in Newfoundland in Canada. She writes: 'The notion of mermaids for me is a reflection on the relationships that sometimes take place between men and women. He is lured by beauty, out of his sea of isolation. She is free of the encumbrance of passion. Her decisions, if she were real in the first place, would be based around herself, so unlike the women who are wives and mothers. The mermaid is nothing more than a fool's paradise.'

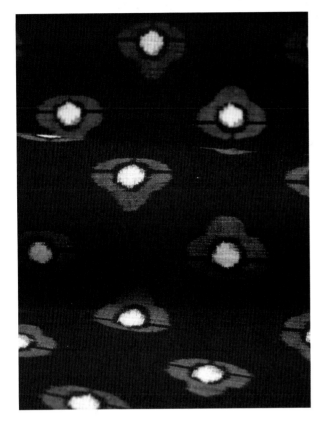

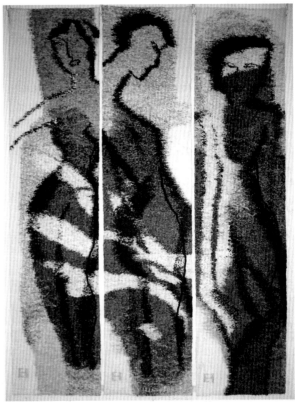

Chinami Ricketts 'Camellia Kimono Yardage' 38 x 1370 cm (15 in x 45 ft). *Kasuri* means 'a splashed pattern' and is the Japanese term for the ikat style of weaving, whereby the yarns are tied with threads in predetermined areas before being dyed, as in this piece, with indigo. It is a complex process that requires the artist to plan in advance exactly where the dyed threads will fall in the weave in order to create her chosen design.

Ehalill Halliste 'Expressionistic' 130 x 35 cm (51 x 13.75 in). Three aspects of women are portrayed in this tapestry triptych, hand woven from wool and flax. The artist comments: 'The work is in a brutal, naturalistic mood. One woman is shown as sexual, one as a mother and the one with a covered face, as a secret. It was inspired by German expressionism.'

Latifa Medjdoub 'Ariel Skirt; Stella Top'. This asymmetrical
royal blue knitted and felted skirt has a series of intriguing holes
in it that might suggest 'secrets underneath' – a notion that
apparently fascinates this former Paris Opera costume designer.

Mary-Clare Buckle 'You' 74 x 65 cm (29 x 25.5 in). Bright colours proclaiming the title word 'You' are held in a grid pattern in this felted piece. The design was inspired by the way in which tiles are used decoratively in the Middle East and North Africa. The artist comments: 'I made a piece of loose felt, cut up the squares, laid that into more wool overlaid with various fibres, cut letters out of "pre-felt", laid them on the squares and felted the whole thing. It is the complement of my piece entitled "Me" [see page 61]. I was partly intending to suggest that, in relationships, two people complement each other – but I also wanted to make the point by using much more subdued colours that you – whoever you are – are never more important than me.'

Chinami Ricketts 'Well Frame Kimono Yardage' 38 x 1370 cm (15 in x 45 ft). Entirely hand woven, this length of *kasuri* fabric is intended for a kimono. The artist uses natural indigo, grown and processed by herself and her husband. She comments: 'When designing and weaving I take into consideration the final sewn design of the kimono as well as the functionality and comfort of the cloth when worn. My kimonos are intended simply to fill the intimate environment of the wearer with joy.'

Ehalill Halliste 'Lady Blue' 110 x 80 cm (43 x 31 in). Thoughtful and enigmatic, this wool and flax handloomed tapestry was inspired by the colour blue and its connotations of peace, spirituality and melancholy. The artist adds: 'The lady is sitting in the evening and thinking back to the day. Sunset brightens her face and wind tousles her hair.'

Marianne Kemp 'Turquoise' 120 x 120 cm (48 x 48 in).
Combining horsehair and cotton, this delicately coloured
woven and knotted piece has an open structure with hairs
peeking out in all directions, giving the weaving a voluminous,
comfortable and flirty feeling, and creating an exciting textural
and visual experience.
(Opposite) 'Turquoise' detail

Latifa Medjdoub 'Peacock'. Inspired by images of nature and the environment, this peacock-blue jacket and skirt have been individually constructed using sculpturally felted merino wool, rayon and Lurex. The designer comments: 'Each collection is one element of an extended process of rethinking and interrogating received images of the human body in nature, as a means of reflecting on the fullest meaning of one's own individuality.'

Deepa Panchamia 100 x 30 cm (36 x 12 in). Shells of all sorts of shapes and sizes were the main source of inspiration for this artist's collection of textile structures and wearable art. This piece combines semi-transparent silk organza and dyed pliable leather by means of energetic pleated waves.

Sofie Brünner 'Metalweave' (top) 42 x 42 cm (16.5 x 16.5 in). Paper and metal yarns are woven together using various techniques including layering, ikat and origami to create this Danish textile designer's fabrics for screens, wallpapers and other interior use.

Laura Thomas 'Landscape Aqua Stripe'. (above) 30 x 60 x 4 cm (12 x 24 x 1.5 in). Original charcoal drawings of the Pembrokeshire landscape in Wales are translated into complex weave structures and woven into a fine cotton and silk cloth on a digital jacquard loom. The final artwork retains the fluid charcoal quality of the original drawings while giving unexpected character to the woven cloth.

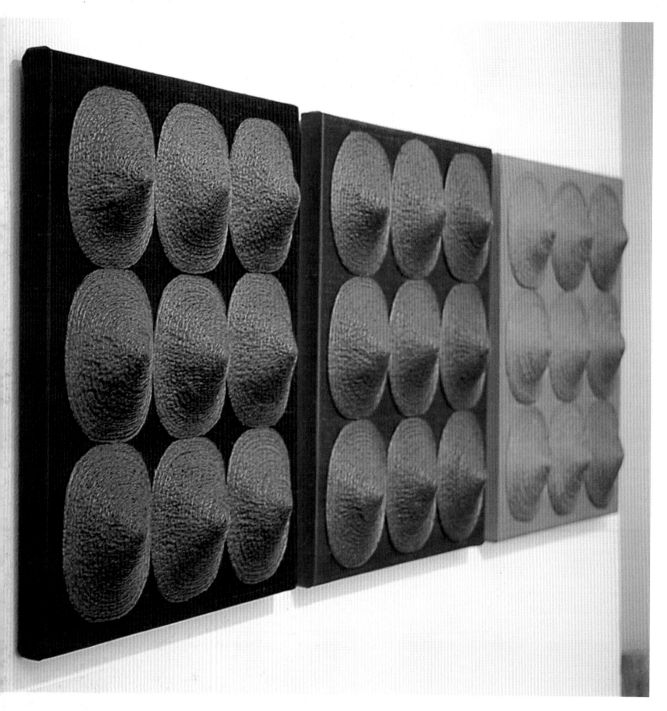

Jenni Cadman 'Blue, Viridian and Teal Peaks' 34 x 34 cm (13.5 x 13.5 in) each panel. Darker toned frames in this wall hanging complement the blue, viridian and teal peaks. The repetitive stitching of silk dupion in a circular motion forms each raised section, leading the artist to describe her piece as being 'inspired by the compulsion to stitch'.

Jeung-Hwa Park 127 x 30 cm (50 x 12 in). Softly rounded textures transform this delicately coloured two-dimensional, machine knitted woollen fabric into a three-dimensional sculpture. Using nuts, seeds and beans, the artist ties tiny bundles over selected sections of the fabric before dyeing and felting the fabric.

Sandra Backlund. Knitted in rib and featuring oversized cables on the sleeves, this dress in bright red wool is a striking example of this artist's approach to her work. She explains: 'The handicraft process and the handmade feeling are very significant. I am interested in almost every traditional handicraft technique. For me it is the absolute challenge. I think it is important that we take responsibility and preserve ancient handicraft techniques, which will die out if we do not carry them forward to a new level.'

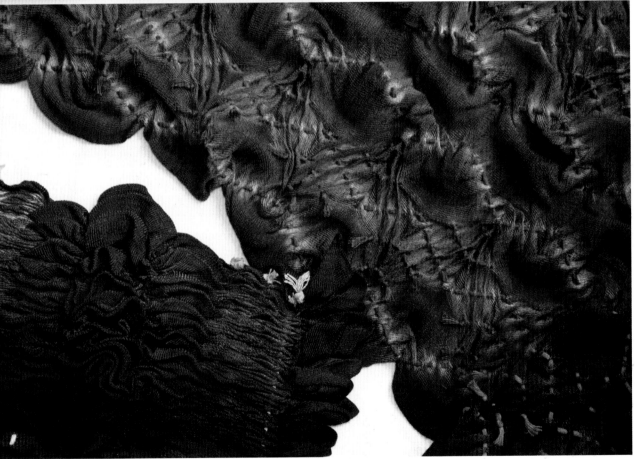

Laura Thomas 'Five Leno Tiles' (top) 12.5 x 12.5 x 3 cm (5 x 5 x 1.25 in). Hand woven cotton and nylon leno fabric, an openwork fabric with the warp threads twisted in pairs before weaving, is encapsulated into polyester resin blocks to create these distinctive and unusual tiles.

Mie Iwatsubo 'Une Ridge' (above) 180 x 30 cm (71 x 12 in). Choosing to work with knitted fabrics for their elasticity and softness, this artist relishes the unpredictability of the resulting patterns. She explains: 'Even though it is time consuming and difficult to mass produce, I depend on this risk factor as it is an essential part of *shibori's* unpredictable beauty. I never hate risks. If anything, I enjoy manipulating these risks.

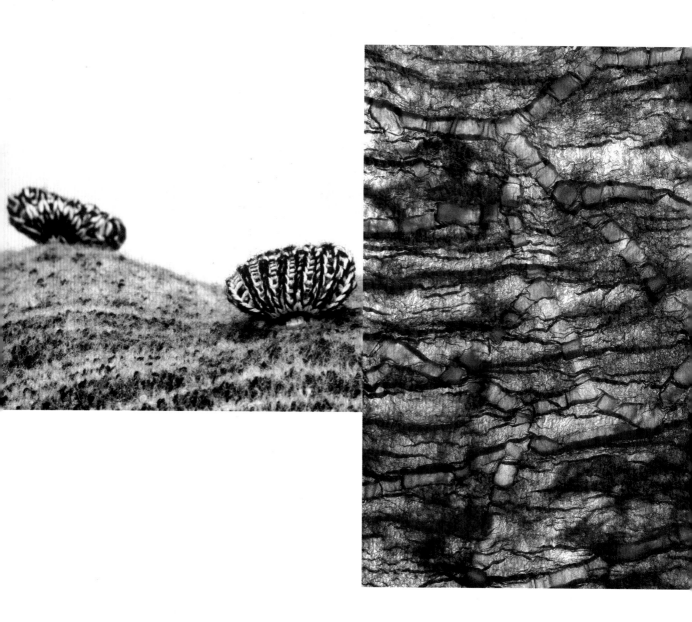

Jeung-Hwa Park 127 x 31 cm (50 x 12.25 in). Knitted, tied and felted bobbles sit like pebbles on top of this wool and silk mix fabric, emphasizing the contrast between surface and projection and convex and concave. Both the front and reverse of these scarves are equally important.

Christine White 'Origins' detail 50 x 128 cm (19.75 x 50.5 in). Many feltmakers are fascinated by backlighting their felt and this artist particularly enjoys illuminating her multi-layered work and playing with variations in depth. The artist comments: 'This hand dyed wool and silk piece is reminiscent of blue-green algae or something seen under a microscope in a biology class. It has a very soothing, watery feel that is somehow familiar at a deep, cellular level.'

Margo Selby 'Scarf from Bubble' 24 x 160 cm (9.5 x 63 in).
Highly textured and woven from silk, this scarf is one of a series
of fabrics that the designer developed on a handloom in her
London studio; they are woven to her requirements by silk mills
in the UK.

Jeung-Hwa Park 127 x 31 cm (50 x 12.25 in). Hazelnuts, chickpeas, beans and other seeds are used to shape the bubble-like textures on this dyed and felted scarf. The artist mixes her own dyes and dips each scarf eight to ten times before she gets the colour she wants. 'It brings life to my work', she says. 'I bring colour and emotion to create balance and harmony.'

Anne Kyyrö Quinn 'Fur Cone' 60 x 60 cm (24 x 24 in). Soft spikes in harmonizing tones of green felt stand up from the surface of this woven woollen cushion, which was inspired by the scales of a fir cone. The artist works in the high-quality felt that has become her signature material. She describes felt as 'a miracle material; as well as being environmentally friendly, tactile, soft and durable, it is easy to work with'.

Melin Tregwynt 'Mondo Gold' 230 cm (90 in) wide. Muted grey-green and gold circles on a neutral background have been produced by a traditional weaving technique called 'double cloth' in this woollen fabric from Wales. This method utilizes two sets of warps and wefts, creating two separate layers of fabric that produce a design when both sets of yarns change position, interlocking the layers at that point.

Mie Iwatsubo 'Momiji' 180 x 35 cm (71 x 13.75 in). This lambswool scarf has been pleated and stitched tightly through small holes in the eyelet pattern of the knitted base fabric. When pleated, the fabric takes on the shape of a *momiji*, which is Japanese for 'maple leaf'. The artist explains: 'While this type of *shibori* pattern is traditionally made by immersing the pleated fabric in a dye bath, I print a discharge dye onto the pleated ridges. This allows the dye to penetrate only the surface of the woollen knit. As a result, the *shibori*-resisted pattern is much sharper than the soft patterns created with immersion dyeing.'

Mie Iwatsubo 'Leheriya' 180 x 40 cm (71 x 16 in). The base
fabric in this shawl has been hand knitted using different colours
and materials before being bound by the *leheriya* technique.
Leheriya is one of the traditional resist techniques from India and
literally means 'waves'. The fabric has been dyed four times,
while tying and untying the *shibori* threads, to produce the
desired chevron pattern.

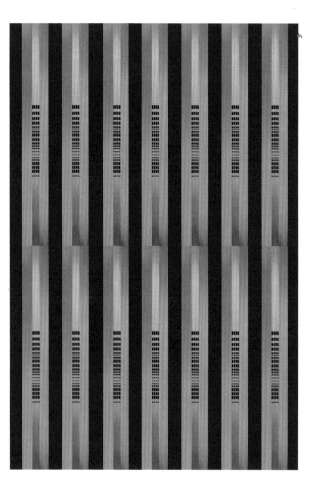

Ptolemy Mann 'Black and Stripe Teal'. Elements of this artist's own woven artwork have been digitally manipulated to produce a textile design that unerringly manages to encapsulate some of her skilful colour values and nuances.

Margo Selby 'Scarf from Silk Bubble' 12 x 160 cm (4.75 x 63 in). An assortment of rich olive, teal, maroon and scarlet hues intermingle in this carefully constructed woven silk scarf, reflecting the designer's love of colour.

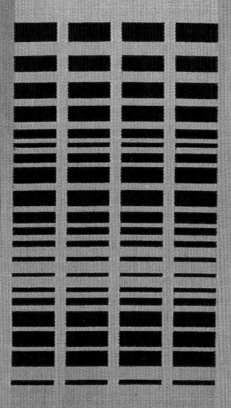

Ptolemy Mann 'Citrine Aqua with Blue Band with Blocks'
50 x 60 cm (19.75 x 24 in). Citrine, aqua and pale sky-blue
mercerized cotton yarns are combined in this textile artwork,
creating a vibrant effect. The woven cloth is carefully stretched
onto a wooden frame, making the work sculptural, architectural,
durable and easy to hang.

Ismini Samanidou 'Wisteria Textiles' 90 x 185 cm (36 x 73 in). Motivated by images of a 300-year-old wisteria plant, these textile wall hangings were created for a curated show at the Hidden Art Cornwall Design Fair at Godolphin House in West Cornwall. The artist comments: 'They were woven on a computerized jacquard loom using cotton, linen, silk and metallic yarns via a combination of designs and weave structures ranging from graduating satins, where the result was almost photographic, to twills that gave a fragmented graphic look.'

Jeung-Hwa Park 127 x 35 cm (50 x 13.75 in). Alternately green and yellow, the surface of this scarf is covered in a plethora of tiny soft protuberances. The artist comments: 'My contemporary knitted fabrics, created by combining knitting, tie-dyeing, stitching and felting are sculptural and textural and simultaneously expand the aesthetics of contemporary knitted fabric and respect the traditional crafts.'

Melin Tregwynt 'Madison Gold' 230 cm (90 in) wide. Softly coloured in shades of olive and gold, this example of a woven double cloth is an example of an old design. It was reintroduced by a small company in Wales in order to preserve traditional skills and knowledge.

Anne Kyyrö Quinn 'Leaf' 50 x 50 cm (19.5 x 19.5 in). Twisted
strips of felt in shades of olive green have been appliquéd
onto woven woollen cloth to create these remarkable textured
cushions. The artist comments: 'This design was inspired by the
dappled light on the forest floor when filtered though the leaf
canopy of high trees. The felt is manipulated in such a way as
to give the impression of dynamic movement of the inanimate
object as one's eye dances over it.'

Mie Iwatsubo 'Crumple' 125 x 15 cm (49 x 6 in). Hand knitted woollen fabric is stitched in order to pleat and gather it before dyeing. After felting, the surface texture achieves the artist's desired crumpled effect. She comments: 'Both sides of the scarf have a different surface and texture – one is crumpled cotton and the other felted wool. I love both of them so I have used both faces alternately in one scarf.'

Ptolemy Mann 'Monolithic Boxes' 50 x 200 cm (19.75 x 78 in).
An installation of six colour-harmonizing, hand woven, stretched
and mounted 'Monolithic Boxes' have been positioned on a
wall in Roast restaurant in London as a direct response to the
architectural surroundings.

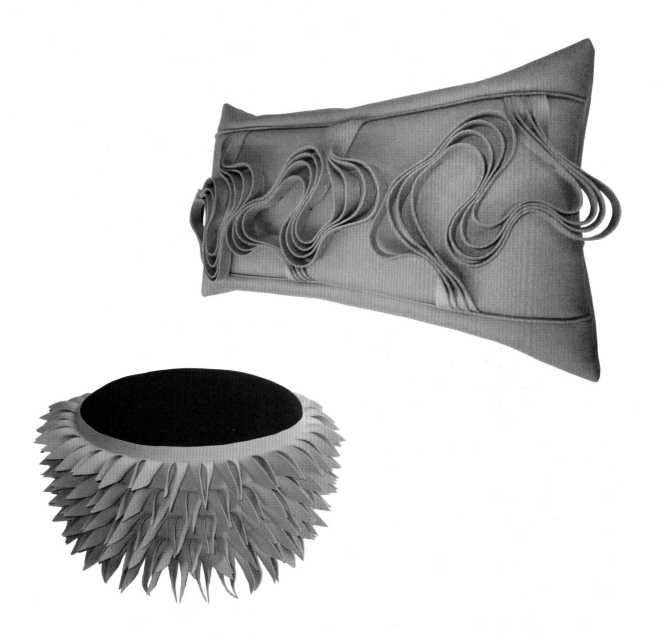

Anne Kyyrö Quinn 'Lola Chair Yellow' 70 x 50 cm (27.5 x 19.75 in). The delicate petals of a newly opened sunflower were the inspiration for this chair, with its sides of curving yellow tips and its seat of dark brown felt. It was created using unusual techniques in order to produce a highly stylized sculptural form. The artist comments: 'Refined lengths of felt work just like other interior textiles, and can even outperform them.'

Anne Kyyrö Quinn 'Origami Cushion' 40 x 60 cm (16 x 24 in). Squiggles of loose blue felt enliven this chartreuse-coloured woven woollen cushion. The artist explains: 'Thicker densities of felt possess unrivalled structure and strength, which makes them perfect for interior architecture.' Because the fibres are so heavily compressed, felt is super strong, has incredible acoustic properties and can be fire-proofed.

Latifa Medjdoub 'Bloom Top; Plant Skirt'. Yellow felt is shaped asymmetrically to produce this skirt, which is teamed with this tasselled white top. The designer uses a range of softly draping fibres such as silk, cashmere and merino wool to produce her unique garments.

Deepa Panchamia 30 x 60 x 40 cm (12 x 24 x 16 in). Accordion pleated waves form this unique moulded headwear. The artist's philosophy towards design is to challenge conventional perspectives of textiles. She comments on her work: 'Through a synthesis of material exploration and my own experimental techniques, I allow my structure to evolve through a series of stages, making the fabric and form equally expressive. My work is solely about reaching this balance – to create an intriguing organic structure that engages notions of aesthetics, rhythm and continuity.'

Ismini Samanidou 'Indigo Map Stripe' 40 x 175 cm (16 x 69 in).
Inspired by images of peeling walls and distressed surfaces,
these fabric prototypes have been hand woven using silk, cotton,
linen, paper and metallic yarns. The fabrics have been overprinted
with metallic and devoré pastes to achieve their distressed look.

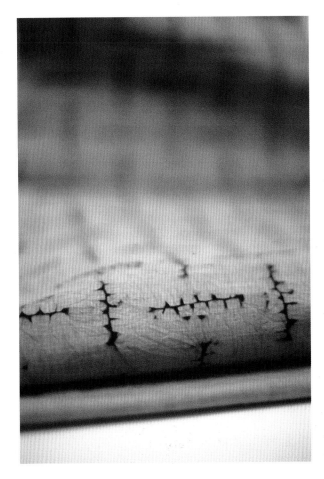

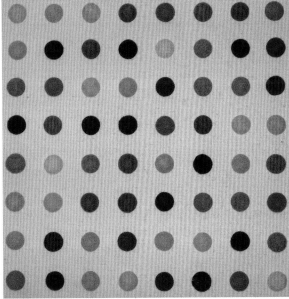

Chinami Ricketts 'Persimmon Lattice Obi Yardage' 33 x 460 cm (13 x 181 in). Hand woven cotton *obi* yardage has been dyed a delicate pinkish-brown with the juice extracted from fruits of the persimmon tree. Known to strengthen the cotton fabrics, this tannin-rich dye has been used for centuries in Japan. After weaving, the artist dyed the fabric using natural indigo and a *shibori* technique.

Lara Hailey 58 x 58 cm (23 x 23 in). Damien Hirst's 'Spot' paintings were the inspiration for this engaging piece consisting of needle-felted balls mounted onto industrial felt. In her own words, Hailey explains: 'I am interested in repetition, authorship and the legacy of craft.'

Deepa Panchamia. Silk dupion and silk organza join in this pleated and pocketed dress. Transparency allows the internal formation to be revealed, creating an engaging relationship between the exterior and interior.

Mie Iwatsubo *'Komasu Shibori'* 170 x 25 cm (67 x 10 in).
Originally inspired by the traditional technique of *komasu shibori,*
which produces small squares, this scarf's base is a knitted fabric
with an eyelet pattern. The artist used cotton threads to stitch
the fabric into tight pleats or gathers before dyeing. The irregular
colour is created through a multiple dye process whereby *shibori*
threads are unravelled three times and, with each new stitching,
a different dye bath is used.

Jeung-Hwa Park 254 x 38 cm (100 x 15 in). The ridged and
elongated shapes that appear in this machine knitted wool and
silk scarf are the result of *shibori* techniques using beans, nuts
or pieces of wood. Once tied into bundles, the whole cloth is
felted. Where the knitted cloth was stretched over an object, it
was prevented from tightening, and so retains its original shape
and structure.

Mary-Clare Buckle 'Outback' 62 x 62 cm (24.5 x 24.5 in). This
piece was inspired by a proposal to produce mock-ups of several
'tourist cliché' pieces on an Australian theme. It combines
transferred digital images with a felted wool background, and
was made by felting the whole piece, cutting into it, laying more
wool behind it and then felting again.

Ingrid Sixsmith 'Transitions' (top) 115 x 148 cm (45 x 58 in). Populated with stylized figures and buildings, this cotton and silk hand woven tapestry is an experimental piece in terms of method and weaving techniques.

Marianne Kemp 'Circles' detail (above) 100 x 80 cm (36 x 31 in). Highly tactile and intriguing, this artist interweaves horsehair with linen or cotton to produce wall panels, installations and window hangings. With years of playful experimentation in shaping the material, she has devised new processes and structures within the weaving process. A standard weaving technique is seldom recognizable in her work. She says: 'It has become my speciality to dream up new exciting effects and shapes.'

Jeung-Hwa Park 127 x 25 cm (50 x 10 in). Using the ancient crafts of resist dyeing and felting, this artist has transformed machine knitted wool into an amazing tactile structure. The artist has this to say about herself and her work: 'Each work has two different aspects: loose, tense; in, out; flat, full. I bring two opposites together in harmony as one piece. It's like me – sometimes I'm American, sometimes I'm Asian.'

Ingrid Tait for Tait & Style 'Mango Pom Stripe Cushion'
40 x 40 cm (16 x 16 in). This striped cushion, made of 100%
lambswool, is first machine knitted to produce panels and then
felted. It is then sent to local outworkers in the Orkney Islands,
Scotland, who sew it up into cushions before making and
attaching the pom-poms.

Prudence Mapstone 'Upstate New York in the Fall' 125 x 68 cm (49 x 26.75 in). Autumnal toned yarns are used to create a jacket that has been knitted and crocheted using natural and synthetic materials. More than 100 separate yarns are incorporated into the garment. The artist comments: 'This piece did not originally have a title, but I wore it when visiting the US one October and felt that it blended in perfectly with the north-eastern fall.'

(Opposite) close-up detail

Anne Kyyrö Quinn 'Tulip' detail 50 x 50 cm (19.75 x 19.75 in).
Somewhat resembling the waving fronds of a sea anemone,
this detail of soft orange felt spikes is from a cushion entitled
'Tulip'. The artist takes inspiration from her love of nature and the
organic regeneration of springtime.

Laura Thomas 'Treescape' 30 x 50 cm (12 x 19.75 in) repeat size. Woven on a digital jacquard loom, the treescape in this silk and cotton mix fabric has a soothing and harmonious atmosphere, no doubt derived from the tranquil countryside of Pembrokeshire, west Wales, which was its original inspiration.

Margo Selby 'Patchwork Cushions' 30 x 60 cm (12 x 24 in).
Glorious and unusual colour combinations have been brought
together to produce these lustrous jacquard woven silk cushions,
with their geometric patterns in light relief.

Jessica Preston 'Rosette Brooches' 9.5 x 9.5 x 2.5 cm (3.75 x 3.75 x 1 in). Using Japanese origami folding techniques as inspiration, these 'Rosette Brooches' become dynamic sculptural patterns that challenge the concept of textiles as flat surfaces.

Melin Tregwynt 'Mondo Red' 230 cm (90 in) wide. Carefully harmonized, the plums and pinks of the spots on this double cloth emphasize the characteristics of the weave. Double cloth fabrics are often quite durable as they have no floating yarns and can make tightly woven structures.

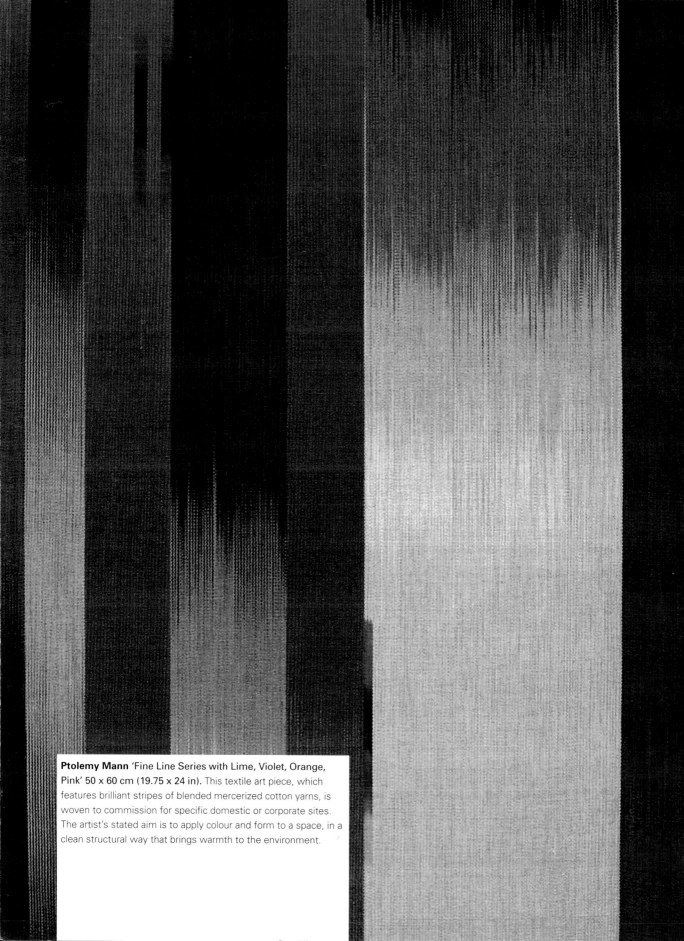

Ptolemy Mann 'Fine Line Series with Lime, Violet, Orange, Pink' 50 x 60 cm (19.75 x 24 in). This textile art piece, which features brilliant stripes of blended mercerized cotton yarns, is woven to commission for specific domestic or corporate sites. The artist's stated aim is to apply colour and form to a space, in a clean structural way that brings warmth to the environment.

Ptolemy Mann 'Portman House Commission' 150 x 350 cm (59 x 138 in). Commissioned for Portman House, London, this large, hand dyed and hand woven textile installation is a colour saturated 'experiential' environment that shows the artist's woven textiles in a powerful and contemporary way.

Anne Kyyrö Quinn 'Origami Cushion Red with Turquoise' 70 x 70 cm (27.5 x 27.5 in). Loops of thick grey wool felt have been twisted and curved before being appliquéd onto the background, giving a strong counterpoint to the dynamic red woven woollen cloth used to create this cushion.

Ptolemy Mann 'Geneva' 40 x 25 x 80 cm (16 x 10 x 31 in).
Woven by hand on a 'dobby' loom, this textile artwork was
created using hand dyed, mercerized cotton yarns, and explores
a sculptural and three-dimensional aspect of the artist's work.

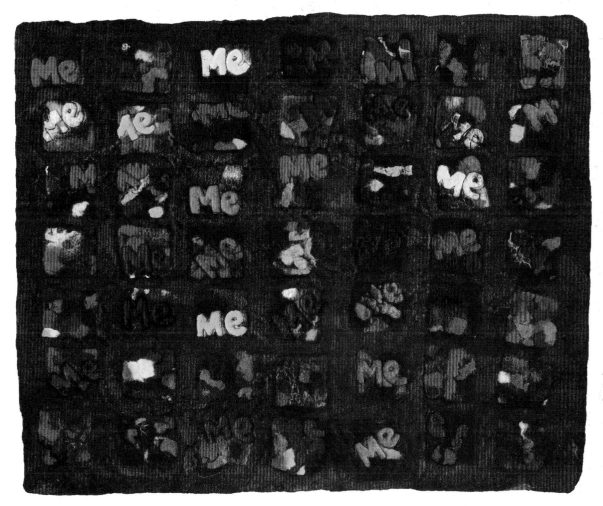

Ingrid Sixsmith 'A&E Homerton' (top) 112 x 226 cm (44 x 89 in). Commissioned for the Accident & Emergency department of Homerton Hospital in the East End of London, this brightly coloured piece explores an urban landscape with two figures depicting racial harmony. The artwork was created as a calming influence and focal point in a very stressful environment. The tapestry is made of wool, cotton, mohair, silk and linen, and was hand woven on a loom.

Mary-Clare Buckle 'Me' (above) 74 x 65 cm (29 x 25.5 in). This felted textile wall hanging, inspired by tile designs from the Islamic tradition, is the companion to the artist's piece entitled 'You' (see page 17). She comments: 'This piece came about by playing with an idea in my head: in this case, the fixation we all have with ourselves, hence my using the piece to scream "Me, Me, Me" in shocking pink.'

Deanne Fitzpatrick 'Squares' (top) 152 x 122 cm (60 x 48 in).
This hooked rug has a contemporary feel, with a pleasing and
harmonious arrangement of colours. The artist comments: 'The
underlying pattern of hit-and-miss blocks is one of the traditional
patterns made in the kitchens of coastal Newfoundland. It
reappears all around the coast as a way of using up what was at
hand.' The rug is highlighted with recycled sari silk yarn, which
gives a rich texture and a shimmer to the mat. The artist plays
up the softness of the lines against the overall hardness of the
pattern of squares.

Saori Okabe 'Penstemon Hat' 14 x 30 cm (5.5 x 12 in).
This multicoloured top hat was made as part of a project on
'Ecology for Nature'. It uses recycled leftover silk yarn from
tie-making.

Prudence Mapstone 'From Midnight to First Light' 95 x
130 cm (37 x 51 in) detail. Subtle tones of mauve, blue and
peach mix together in this 'freeform' hand crocheted and knitted
cape. The artist writes: 'Inspired by the changes in light just
before the crack of dawn, this award-winning cape was created
for the theme of "Outback Australia".' The yarns used are 4-ply
wool, mohair, cotton and Lurex, and the garment took almost
eight months to complete.

Laura Willits 'Camp Cernunnos' 33 x 45 cm (13 x 18 in). This
artist creates haunting images of night landscapes, showing
the sudden, luminous glow of lamplight on a tree or a building.
Sometimes these images are of a real place, and sometimes
they are of somewhere she has visited in her mind. The images
are woven using thousands of beads in hundreds of colours,
which are then woven into a heavy fabric.

Christine White 'Cocoon' 50 cm (19.75 in) long. Unusually, the artist chose to use the *shibori* technique of *arashi* to create this woollen three-dimensional piece. It was evidently a challenge to apply the technique, which involved wrapping the thick, hard piece of felt around a cylindrical column before dyeing and manipulating it to produce the desired texture and sharp lines.

Ptolemy Mann 'Violet, Indigo Dynamic' 50 x 60 cm (19.75 x 24 in). Brilliantly coloured with violet and indigo morphing into mustard, this dynamic mercerized cotton textile artwork has been hand dyed and woven on an upright dobby loom and then stretched over a wooden frame to give the work an architectural arrangement.

Ptolemy Mann 'Indigo, Violet Dynamic Stripe' Digital print.
Using elements of her unique woven textiles, this artist has
been developing repeating geometric patterns via a computer,
thus evoking the handmade quality and unique blending of colour
in the more commercially viable form of digital printing.

Christine White 'Night Ocean' (top) 40 x 60 cm (16 x 24 in).
A dark and mysterious piece, this hand dyed merino-wool felted piece conjures up the thought of drifting out on the open ocean at night, which is at once supremely beautiful and terrifying.

Deanne Fitzpatrick 'Islands' 112 x 142 cm (44 x 56 in).
Overlapping lands surrounded by swirls of sea were the inspiration for this hooked rug. The artist comments: 'I love barrens, having spent hours on them as a child either berry-picking or fishing. To me they are immensely interesting, and I have found that wool, with its many subtle shades and slight differences of texture, works well to express them.' She goes on to explain how wool gives a sculptural quality to a piece even if that intention was not there in the first place.

Sandra Backlund. This garment is knitted in an oversized open-lace stitch and is another example of this designer's unique approach to her work. She comments: 'I am really fascinated by all the ways you can highlight, distort and transform the natural silhouette of the body with clothes and accessories. In my opinion clothes are the most democratic form of art. Something everyone does relate to consciously or unconsciously.'

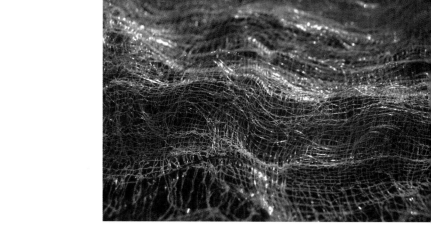

Liz Clay. Pebble-shaped balls of felted wool and silk have been resist dyed with indigo to form this unusual neckpiece.

Charlotte Grierson 'Seascape' 60 x 125 cm (24 x 49 in). Glistening like the sunlight on the surface of the sea, this experimental hand woven triple cloth uses nylon monofilament, enamelled copper wire and high twist silk to reflect the light differently. Once woven, the piece was washed, allowing the twisted silk to manipulate the cloth and create the sculptured effect.

Sue Lawty 'Mesh' detail 300 x 100 cm (10 x 4 ft). This delicate piece is exhibited in Gallery 101 in the Victoria & Albert Museum, London. It was created using clear thread with pieces of coral knotted where the threads crossed over. The artist explains: 'The resulting "fabric" is a series of floating marks which, when seen against a white background, become virtually invisible. As the piece is approached it suddenly pops into focus, a bit like a spider's web might.'

Katherine Maxwell. Loom knitted, cotton mesh fabric incorporates hand spun interweavings to create this unique garment. The artist finds inspiration in 'the texture of the materials, which are not always yarns, but sometimes packing twine, fishing line or copper wire.'

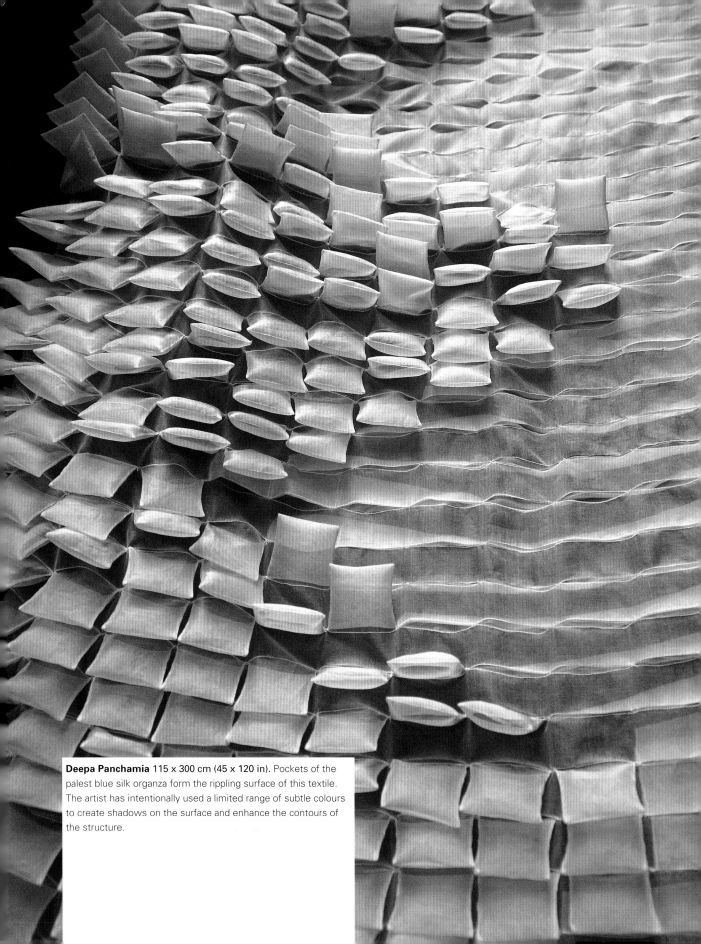

Deepa Panchamia 115 x 300 cm (45 x 120 in). Pockets of the palest blue silk organza form the rippling surface of this textile. The artist has intentionally used a limited range of subtle colours to create shadows on the surface and enhance the contours of the structure.

Sandra Backlund. White wool knitted into rolls and tubes are then assembled to make this unusual garment. The artist always works with the human body as a starting point. She comments: 'I construct my designs from a lot of small pieces which I attach to each other in different ways to discover the shape that I want. In that sense, I guess you can say that I approach fashion more like a sculptor then a tailor.'

Angelika Klose 'Luna'. Using the unusual material of banana leaf fabric, this artist creates her hats by working more like a sculptor than a milliner. This hat was influenced by the halos featured in early Christian iconography as well as the image of Florence Nightingale, the famous nurse of the Crimean War era.

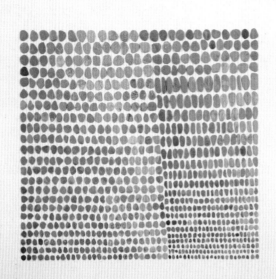

Deepa Panchamia 120 x 30 x 40 cm (48 x 12 x 16 in). By transforming fabric into a three-dimensional structure with inventive pleating and manipulation, the artist has created a silk organza and leather 'sculptural tower', which is detailed yet controlled and energetic yet coherent.

Sue Lawty 'Slant' 58 x 58 cm (29 x 29 in). Here, natural stones on gesso make a mesmerizing pattern. The artist explains: 'I often choose to draw in monochrome and use colour very sparingly in tapestry, yet I find myself becoming increasingly intrigued by the range and qualities of colour found on a seemingly grey beach. Only after hours spent crawling around the coastline, nose to the ground, do the shades and tones become evident within the grey swathes'.

Ismini Samanidou 'Thalassa' 90 cm (36 in) wide. Inspired by images of the sea and waves, this fabric prototype for interior textiles has been woven on a computerized jacquard loom using cotton and paper yarns. Variations in the weft density were achieved by manually changing the weft ratio while weaving.

Ismini Samanidou 'The Cuadra Chair'. This unique chair is the
first collaboration between this textile designer and furniture
designer John Miller. Both are based at University College
Falmouth in Cornwall, England. They were able to design the
fabric and the chair together rather than applying an existing fabric
to a new chair or designing a special fabric for an existing chair.

Ismini Samanidou 'The Cuadra Chair' detail. The artist comments on her creative process: 'My process starts by taking photographs of natural forms and textures. I then develop them into designs by applying weave structures to the patterns and make a selection of yarns in response to the photographs. Operating the loom enables me to respond to the fabric as it is being made; changing the design and the yarns intuitively. Thus the resulting fabrics retain a very personal hands-on and considered feel.'

Christine White 'Valances' 43 x 86 cm (17 x 34 in) each. White Wensleydale wool mixed with Blue-faced Leicester locks have been used to create these delicate hanging structures. The artist comments: 'Hand felting high-quality cobweb felt takes much skill. Although it's fairly easy to produce an artistically interesting felt with a lot of random holes, it is much more difficult to make an even, consistent texture that is still as sheer as possible.' She goes on to explain how some feltmakers use a power sander to make cobweb felt as the vibration speeds the process, but she feels that it also removes the intimate dialogue between the artist and her medium. Therefore, expert feltmakers use only their hands to slowly and deliberately coax the fibres together into a perfect, sheer sheet.

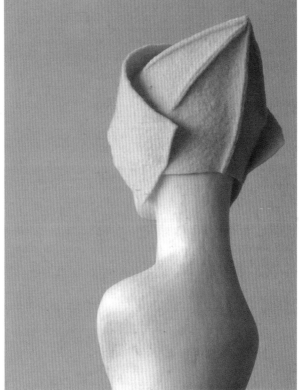

Angelika Klose 'Florence'. Influenced by helmets from the Middle Ages, and those of Japanese Samurai warriors, this remarkable hat was formed from pieces of fabric, the shapes emerging from the sculptural qualities of the material.

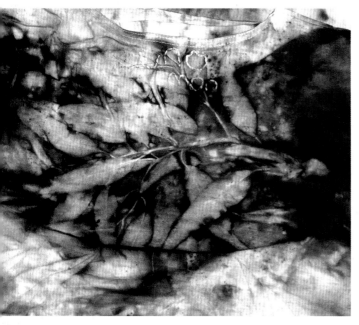

India Flint. This is a detail from a eucalyptus printed merino jersey shirt that features the artist's special ecoprint watercolour technique. She explains: 'I only work with natural fibres. Most of these I source second hand, although I do allow myself to use new silk and wool, as both of these come from renewable sources. All of my dyes are made from plants and no toxic chemical adjuncts are used.'

Katherine Maxwell. Inspired by Medieval chain-mail tunics, this loom knitted garment is made from linen and cotton yarns using a simple, almost primitive construction technique. She comments: 'I use a bulky knitter which I have stripped down to leave just the bed and carriage with no tension rods, punch patterns or any computer gadgets.'

Charlotte Grierson 'Exploration' 56 x 135 cm (22 x 53 in).
Resembling a panorama of shimmering sands, this inventive
hand woven double and triple cloth uses enamelled copper
wire, nylon monofilament and high twist silk in its construction.
The artist comments: 'This was an experimental piece which
explored creating a tension between the behaviour of the
materials and the weave structure of the cloth. The inspiration
came from coastal landscapes and seascapes.'

Lene Nordfeldt Iversen 'With love from Kökar' detail 70 x 100 cm (27.5 x 36 in). Hand woven on a computer-controlled loom, this viscose, polyester and nylon textile contains a hidden text saying 'Nature is beautiful' and is an example of an autostereogram, which is a pattern designed to trick the brain into perceiving a three-dimensional image in a two-dimensional scene. The artist comments: 'In order to perceive three-dimensional shapes in these autostereograms, the brain must overcome the normally automatic coordination between focusing and coordination.'

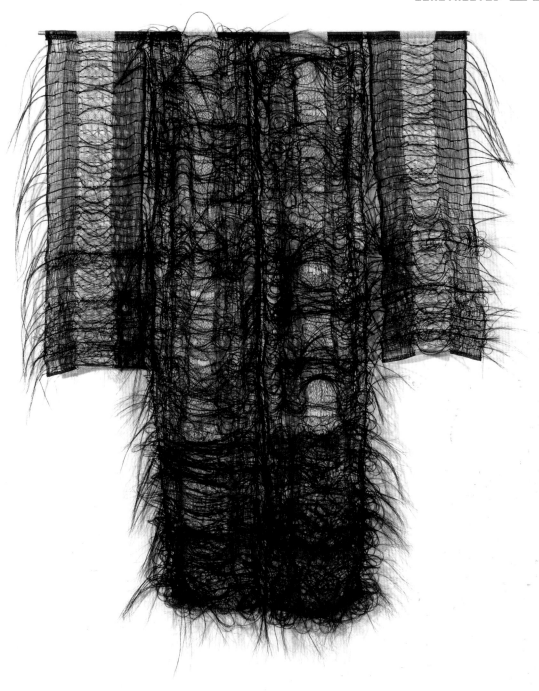

Marianne Kemp 'Kimono' 120 x 150 cm (48 x 59 in). Small bunches of horsehair have been interwoven and knotted with cotton and wool to make this wall hanging. Japanese pen drawings and the crossing of thick and thin lines inspired the piece. The artist says: 'The open texture, with hairs jumping out, creates beautiful shadows, making their own drawings on the wall or floor.'

DYED, PRINTED AND PAINTED

This section focuses on colour and its manipulation via innovative or conventional dye, print or paint techniques to produce patterns that are inherently pleasing to the eye. These featured designs are predominantly concerned with two-dimensional decoration for the home, apparel or contract markets.

To create the designs, the majority of artists have used screen-printing, and have hand printed their work, though some examples have been commercially screen-printed. A number of designers have produced their designs digitally, a process that allows for finer detail and a much larger colour range, and one pioneering artist has even combined digital-printing with batik, hand rendering and dyeing to produce her unique art pieces.

Several of the textile designs featured here utilize additional processes such as foiling, crimp paste and devoré to achieve unusual surface effects, and some artists have painted directly onto silk with dyes or pigments using gutta, wax resist or rozome techniques. There are also examples of innovative designers who have originated printing methods of their own, such as 'eco-printing' and 'deconstructed' printing.

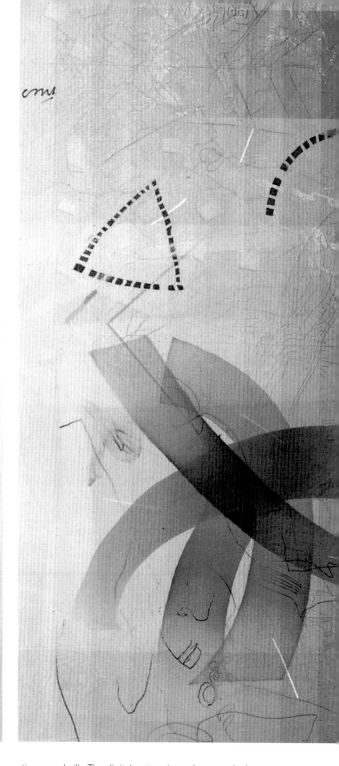

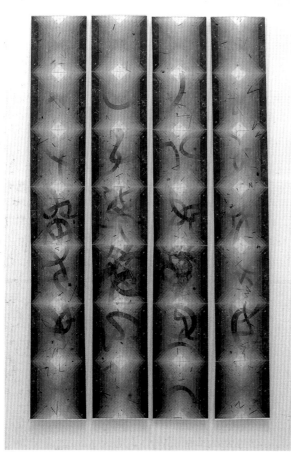

Pat Hodson 'Blue on Blue' 280 x 160 cm (110 x 63 in). Blue shapes appear to hover within a blue space in this extraordinary large and complex tissue paper and *habotai* silk piece. The artist comments: 'The deepest blue is seen in the batik shape, which dominates and seems to float on the surface, but is in fact embedded beneath the surface, between the layers of tissue and silk. The digital pattern in each square is the same, but the collage and batik in each square are unique.' The digital print combines computer-manipulated and -generated drawings, which have been developed from scans of watercolours, maps, drawings and photo-organic materials.

Pat Hodson 'Blue on Blue' detail. This close-up detail demonstrates the artist's examination of the way that old and new interact, and the qualities of digital colour in relation to dyed colour. She explains: 'The pieces I make combine new and old textile technologies. Illusory computer images interact with the reality of the tactile collage surface, the colour of the dyed image with digitally-printed colour, and hand drawn marks with computer marks.'

Pat Hodson 'Blue on Blue' detail. This single page from the large 'Blue on Blue' piece combines traditional collage and textile materials with digital technology. The result is a very strong, tactile and flexible material that is translucent. The artist explains: 'Each piece is made by a lamination technique whereby silk and tissue are collaged with cellulose glue. Drawings and dyed resist pieces are embedded within the collage. Stitch and wax resist is then applied to the surface, and then the whole is digitally printed. After printing and drying, the piece is waxed and stitched together.'

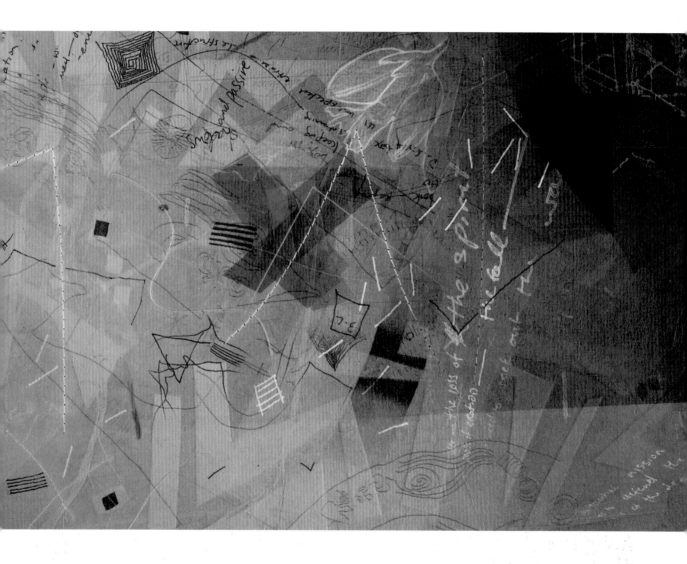

Pat Hodson 'Blue on Blue' detail. The artist explains: 'Tissue and silk are layered, and embedded within the layers are fragments which might be hidden or revealed through interplay between the translucent surface and the layers beneath. The result is a tactile multilayered surface, over which is printed a digital image. The spatial illusion within the digital image is made up from "suggested" marks, and textures – an illusory drawing on screen which interacts with the actual texture over which it is printed. Each will be affected and be changed by the other.'

Sarah Pearson Cooke. The designer uses indigo in combination with *itijime* (clamp resist) and *arashi* (pole wrapped) shibori techniques to create spotted and striped patterns.

Carole Waller 'Feather Coat'. Made from indigo blue silk organza with a silk satin dress, this unique ensemble has been hand painted onto the constituent parts of the garment before being sewn together.

Rowland Ricketts 180 x 180 cm (71 x 71 in). Designed as a *noren* or traditional Japanese partition, this *katazone* (paste-resist), hemp textile is dyed using natural indigo that the artist has grown and processed himself. He explains: 'My *noren* is also a screen that captures and filters the shifting light and air of the space, bringing life and movement to the cloth, and reflecting back the transitory experience with its presence.'

Cressida Bell 'Ibis' 60 x 58 cm (24 x 23 in). Drawn with an enviable sureness of touch, these ibis are truly delightful. Each line is significant and indispensable, whilst portraying a certain wry humour. The birds were subsequently collaged onto the randomly-spotted cobalt blue background.

Marie Wright 'Landscape, Birkrigg' 45 x 154 cm (18 x 60.5 in) **each panel.** Archaeological finds and parch marks left by ancient settlements are the unusual inspiration for this printed and hand painted screen.

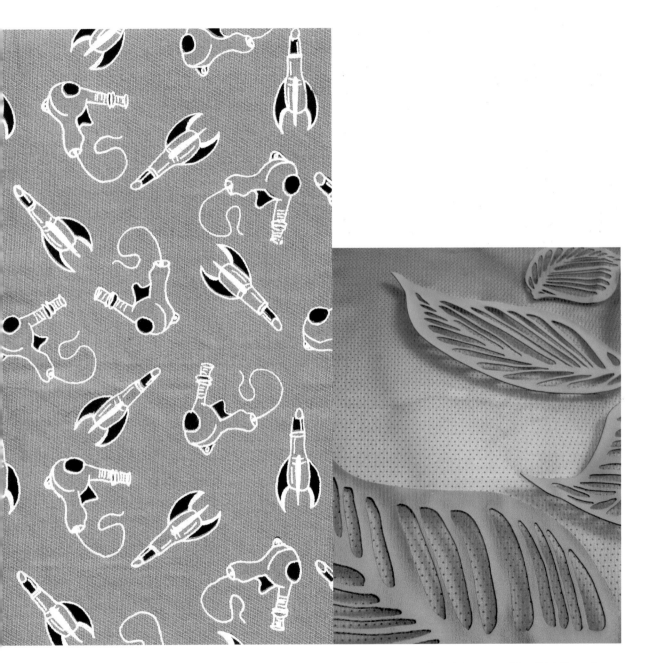

Panayiota Panayiotou 'Lipstick and Hairdryer Ray Gun Fabric'. Clearly inspired by designs from the 1950s, this hand screen-printed cotton fabric combines images of rockets with a fantasy image of a hairdryer doubling up as a ray gun.

Laura Mackay 'Blue Lycra' 60 x 41 cm (24 x 16 in). Tiny polka dots printed onto silk organza are enhanced via appliquéd laser cut Lycra leaf shapes in this brightly coloured, experimental fabric sample.

Laura Mackay 'Blue Devoré' 41 x 45 cm (16 x 18 in).
Devoré, also known as 'burn out', produces this design of a natural form set against a screen-printed background of dots. Devoré is a popular technique with textile designers, as it produces a contrast in texture between the sharply defined translucent silhouettes of the devoréd design motif and the soft raised pile of the background fabric.

Timorous Beasties 'Oriental Tree' 180 cm (70 in) wide.
Unmistakably influenced by Japanese decorative designs, the repeating pattern of these delicate pine tree silhouettes provides a soothing backdrop for urban living.

Laura Mackay 'Branch' 30 x 45 cm (12 x 18 in). Digitally produced, this textile design of overlaid organic forms is reminiscent of a cyanotype print, a light-sensitive photographic printing process that gives a Prussian blue print.

Jason Black 22 x 51 cm (8.5 x 20 in). This artist has been fortunate to encounter various underwater locations in Malaysia and the Red Sea, and has carefully planned this piece to create an attractive and detailed reef scene with a feeling of depth, perspective and movement. He comments: 'I spent countless hours observing this wonderful world and just as many hours on dry land developing the technique I use in my paintings. I use the *gutta serti* technique, which has always been my preferred method since first painting on silk. I use only clear *gutta* to restrict the flow of colour, steam fix paints and water.'

Walkiria Caramico 'Peixe Fish' 100 x 100 cm (36 x 36 in). This Brazilian artist uses *gutta* (a solution that penetrates the fabric to provide an outline and helps prevent dyes from running into each other) and vibrantly coloured dyes to evoke a contemplative mood in her depiction of fishes and coral.

Jane Keith. Featuring a large textile screen-printing table, this is a studio shot of some of this artist's work in progress and demonstrates how hand screen-printed work operates with the fabric being pinned or taped to the table's backing cloth. The artist comments: 'In the studio, you can see small panels pinned up on the wall behind the print table, which are sketch panels on silk that I make before working up a hanging to scale. I treat them like sketchbook pages on silk, experimenting with colours, imagery, scale and composition.'

Natasha Marshall 'Calypso' 137 cm (54 in) **wide.** Inspired by scuba diving trips taken by the designer in the Caribbean and Australia, these cushions are screen-printed onto a cotton and linen mix using vat dyes for light fastness and durability. The designer comments: 'The vibrancy and beauty of the colours and the fluidity of the marine environment are truly breathtaking. I wanted to bring a feeling of this stunning setting into an interior through my printed fabric collection Calypso and its coordinating wallpaper range Atlantis.'

Sari Syväluoma 'Turquoise Forest' 30 x 50 cm (12 x 19.75 in). Spanning the design culture of Finland and the restrained sensibilities of Norway, this screen-printed 100% linen cushion has real character. The designer comments: 'I find inspiration from colours, light, both everyday life and holidays. "Think of your home as your universe, filled with the things you love, things that tell the story of you".'

Jason Black 68 x 43 cm (26.75 x 17 in). Diving and observing the creatures of the coral reefs off the island of Koh Tao, situated in the Gulf of Thailand, led this artist to portray some of the remarkable scenes he saw in a series of paintings on silk. This painting includes several tree-like gorgonian corals, an emperor angelfish and a striped lionfish.

Dorothy Bunny Bowen 'Dun 1, Scotland' 41 x 51 cm (16 x 20 in). This brooding study of a Scottish mountain, produced by the *rozome* process, has a powerful energy. The artist observes: 'Many of the rulers of the ancient Kingdom of Dalriada are buried in the shadow of Dun I, over on the sacred Isle of Iona, where the Book of Kells was likely written. Such introspection has revealed in me a strong bonding to mountains, in a specific as well as a general sense. Now I understand why it has always been there whence I looked for inspiration, for hope, for solace. And why I cannot imagine living where the world is flat.'

Dionne Yang 'Digital Image' 50 x 50 cm (19.75 x 19.75 in). This design consists of an array of understated colours, rhythmical hand sketches and quirky paintings drawn from the artist's imagination and interaction with nature, and then digitally-printed onto silk chiffon.

Kerr Grabowski 'Martha's Bad Day'. Dynamic stripes form the collar of this long monoprinted silk coat with its animated lining. The artist comments: 'This is a reversible coat so that "Martha" can be worn on the outside if desired. "Martha" is a bit peeved at always being inside the coat so is sticking out her tongue and going…'

Design Team Nya Nordiska 'Prisma' 300 cm (120 in) wide. Lively radiating lines with their centres of blue or yellow coloured squares make this sheer devoréd polyester and viscose mix fabric appear very animated, while maintaining a certain stylishness.

Laura Bissonnet 30 x 20 cm (12 x 8 in). Lucienne Day, the influential British textile designer of the post-war period, was the inspiration for this paper design of lilies. The artist subsequently digitally manipulated her design to produce framed pieces and greetings cards as well as developing it into fabric wall hangings.

Ingrid Sixsmith 'Linklaters' 450 x 300 cm (180 x 120 in). Created for the vestibule of an office in the City of London, this digitally-printed silk triptych was inspired by the soothing but light enhancing depiction of rocks and water. The artist comments: 'Nature provides a universal language in an artificial environment and it can be enhanced in order to uplift spirits in a busy corporate environment.'

Laura Mackay 'Turquoise Silk' 45 x 37 cm (18 x 14.5 in). Dyed turquoise silk viscose is screen-printed with a devoré dot before pink laser-cut velvet branch shapes are bonded to it in this experimental fabric sample.

Dru Cole 'Weld and Indigo' 33 x 115 cm (13 x 45 in) each. Weld and indigo are two of the oldest natural dyestuffs to have been in continual use. They combine in this subtly dappled silk scarf, by means of an exhaust dye bath and an *arashi shibori* technique. The resulting patterns are surprisingly difficult to reproduce!

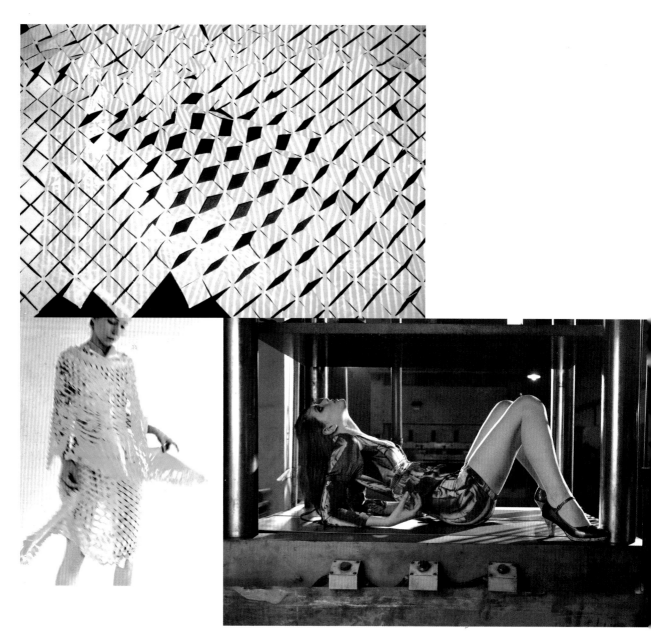

Lidia Muro 'Green Laser Cut Fabric' dress and detail 40 x 30 cm (15.75 x 12 in). An exploration of the possibilities of geometrics linked to movement, this cotton fabric is laser cut with a pattern of repeated squares. The fabric opens and closes according to the movements of the person wearing it, being flat when stationary and becoming three-dimensional at other times.

Yu Chu Amanda Yuen. Digitally-printed to resemble pleated and distressed fabric, this jumpsuit forms part of a research project into families of designs.

Christina Strutt for Cabbages and Roses 'Blue Hatley Natural' **145 cm (57 in) wide.** Inspired by vintage fabrics found at antique fairs and markets, this screen-printed cotton and linen fabric, with a design of faded over-blown roses, conjures up a tranquil air of understated charm.

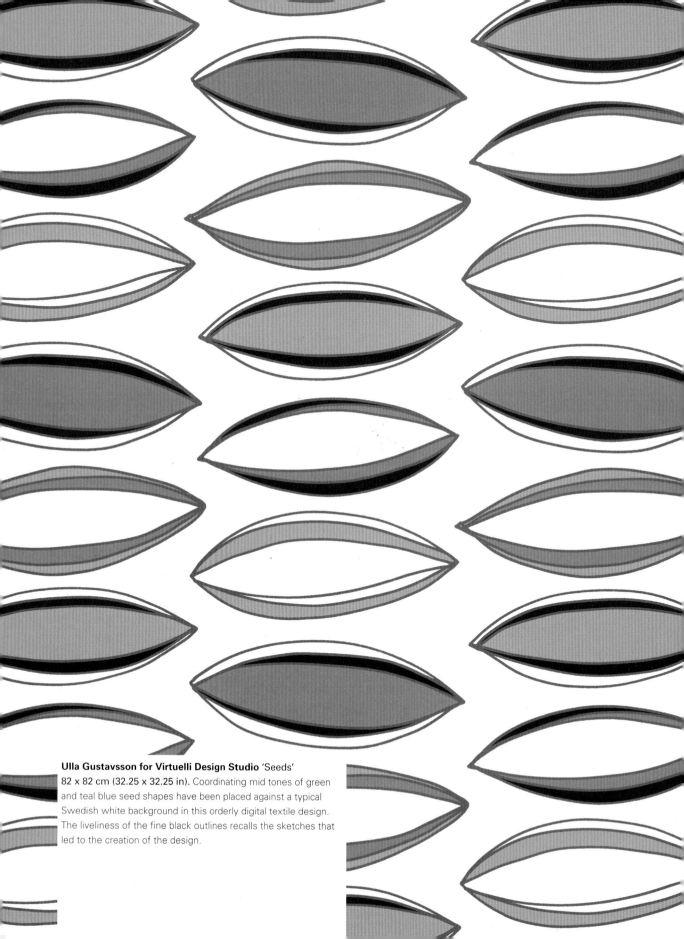

Ulla Gustavsson for Virtuelli Design Studio 'Seeds'
82 x 82 cm (32.25 x 32.25 in). Coordinating mid tones of green
and teal blue seed shapes have been placed against a typical
Swedish white background in this orderly digital textile design.
The liveliness of the fine black outlines recalls the sketches that
led to the creation of the design.

Hannah McMahon for Zedzz 32 x 32 cm (12.5 x 12.5 in).
Referencing Japanese prints and Gustav Klimt paintings, this
screen-printed silk fabric for wrap dresses and kimonos has a
melancholy palette of the type found in Art Nouveau textiles
– smoky purple, teal and grey.

Ilkka Timonen for Virtuelli Design Studio 'Hops' 66 x 66 cm (26 x 26 in). Crisp and clear-cut, this digital textile design portrays the unmistakable vigour of the hop plant as it winds inexorably upwards.

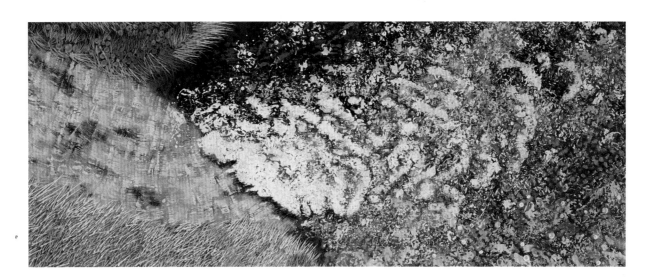

Robin Paris 165 x 67 cm (65 x 26 in). This artist has a fascination with portraying the spirit of the rivers and streams of Cornwall, on the south west coast of England. She uses wax resist and sgraffito techniques to transfer her designs onto fabric.

Marion Piffaut 'Transformable Fabric' 45 x 45 cm (18 x 18 in).
Conceived under the title of 'Transformable Fabric', the designer
explains the idea behind this project: 'I created a range of scarves
that change colours when you wash them, for example the
brown and red trees change with time and seasons to green and
yellow, or you can discover some text underneath a colour when
you wash your scarf.'

Saori Okabe 50 x 30cm (19.75 x 12 in). Gentle foliage and floral motifs in harmonizing tones of green, gold and grey combine in this design for a textile inspired by the artist's childhood memories of Japan.

Ulla Gustavsson for Virtuelli Design Studio 'Dill' 45 x 45 cm (18 x 18 in). Reproduced onto textiles, napkins and mugs by Hemtex AB, Sweden, this pattern of dill seeds has enough irregularity in its detail and composition to delight and engage the eye.

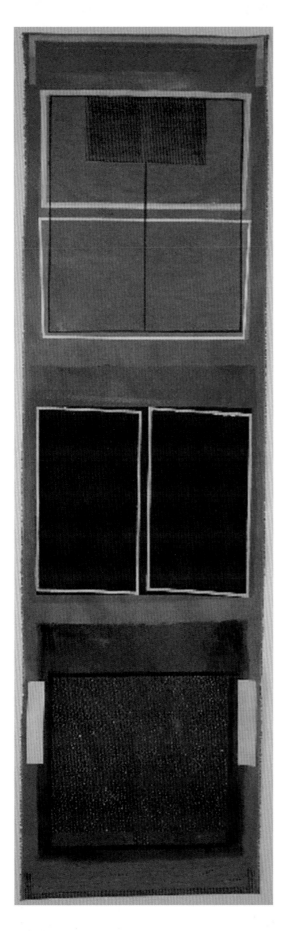

Sally Greaves-Lord 'The Serpentine' 206 x 59 cm (81 x 23.25 in).
Evoking a contemplative mood, this large and richly patterned
wall hanging of dyed, spun silk has been entirely hand painted
using pigments, dyes and discharge agents.'

Cressida Bell 'Leaves' 140 x 120 cm (55 x 47 in). Leafy branches are interspersed with berries and surrounded by a precisely delineated border pattern of dots and dashes in this hand painted gouache design for a rug.

Timorous Beasties 'Ig Light Green'. A green iguana moves in to capture its prey – a butterfly – in a detailed and somewhat macabre design from this renowned Glasgow design team.

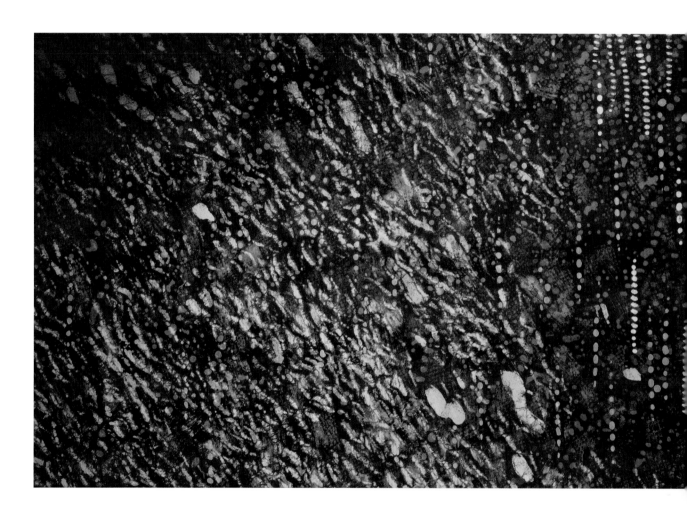

Robin Paris 'De Lank Camel' detail 77 x 77 cm (30 x 30 in).
Captivated by the ripples, light and reflections on the water
surface, this artist works with wax resist using found materials
and home-made tools such as chicken wire and bicycle-chain
wheels to portray some of the qualities of the Cornish rivers that
she so admires.

Brian Barratt 'Roses, Ornaments, Ferrets and Moths' 62
x 62 cm (24.5 x 24.5 in). These images have been digitally
manipulated and compiled to create this unusual printed textile.
The artist has drawn and gathered images with the intention
of creating something beautiful out of what could be initially
thought of as chaos. He remarks: 'My textiles incorporate hand-
and digital-printing techniques and feature drawings which are
feminine but quirky, and at times explore a darker angle. My
inspirations include British wildlife and taxidermy.'

India Flint 'Lunanova' 90 x 150 cm (36 x 59 in). Eco-printing is a process discovered by the artist, who in this example used eucalyptus leaves. This hand felted woollen wrap has a yellow background obtained from a pre-mordant bath of *Oxalis pes-caprae*, or soursob. The eucalyptus species used included *Eucalyptus maculata, sideroxylon* and *cinerea*, which produce dyes that are substantive on protein fibres (such as wool and silk), meaning that colour can be fixed without the use of chemical mordants.

Suzanne Silk A foiled image of a crane adds an oriental essence to the back of this multi-layered, silk organza kimono.

Els van Baarle 'De Tijd is Om' ('The Time is For…') 100 x 300 cm (36 x 120 cm). This long length of dyed, discharged and screen-printed cotton fabric uses fibre-reactive dyes in their characteristic turquoise to golden-yellow range, inevitably producing this particular range of mid tone greens. Afterwards, phrases in Dutch have been overprinted to give a personal meaning to the piece.
(Above left) detail from the print

Barbara Fidoe 'Passage' 112 x 180 cm (44 x 71 in). Architectural
in style and ambiance, this textile has been created in response
to the colour, space and structure of the artist's surrounding
environment. Everyday situations and visual memories have
been gathered and expressed in the designs.

Rose de Borman 'Orange Silk' 38 x 28 cm (15 x 11 in).
Conceived as an unusual homage to the lost pets buried in an old
French cemetery, this screen-printed silk sample includes various
images inspired by strange memorials the artist discovered there.

Jane Keith 'Cadmium Medina' 135 x 195 cm (53 x 77 in).
Cadmium yellow is the main colour used for this striking hand
painted and screen-printed wall hanging inspired by a research
trip to Essaouira, a small coastal town in Morocco. Subtle
colouring and texture have been introduced into selected areas
by means of a complex layering technique involving different
dyes, pigments and processes.

Sharon Ting 100 x 200 cm (39.25 x 78.75 in). These spotted and striped scarves are devoré printed onto a silk viscose mix using the same subtle harmonizing colour scheme of mustard, terracotta, teal and brown to create a mellow mood.

Sharon Ting 50 x 200 cm (19.5 x 39.25 in). This artist uses print to give a three-dimensional look to her creations. Movement is also a theme, where fine textures and small repeated dots work their way into the larger geometric shapes.

Dorothy Bunny Bowen 'Fire Study' 36 x 46 cm (14 x 18 in).
Dramatic and energetic, this powerful study of fire was created
via the complex *rozome,* or wax resist, process. The artist
comments on her inspiration: 'In the summer of 2003 I was in
the Rio Grande valley in Texas when a major fire started. It was
traumatic to be in the choking smoke as people were being
evacuated from their homes, and I subsequently created several
images inspired by this experience.'

Laura-Jane O'Kane. Vividly coloured flower prints overprinted
by a bold black rose design give a lively and decidedly
Mediterranean feeling to an experimental hand and screen-
printed silk satin dress fabric.

Barbara Fidoe 'Moment' 68 x 75 cm (26.75 x 29.5 in).
Distressed areas of colour crossed by vigorous stripes have
been created on this velvet textile using a combination of hand
painting and screen-printing, discharge and devoré processes, to
build up and remove layers of colour and texture.

Zakee Shariff 'Star Guitar' 120 cm (47.25 in) wide. The artist was inspired to create this fashion fabric by the guitars belonging to her musician husband. She uses a regular repeat of differently shaped guitars to form this screen-printed design.

Caitlin Hinshelwood 'Donkey Express Calico' 21 x 21 cm
(8.25 x 8.25 in). Donkeys carrying letters are the unusual motifs
in this screen-printed fabric, inspired by the artist's affection for
the postal service and her admiration for the ephemera, posters
and artwork of the Postal Heritage archive.

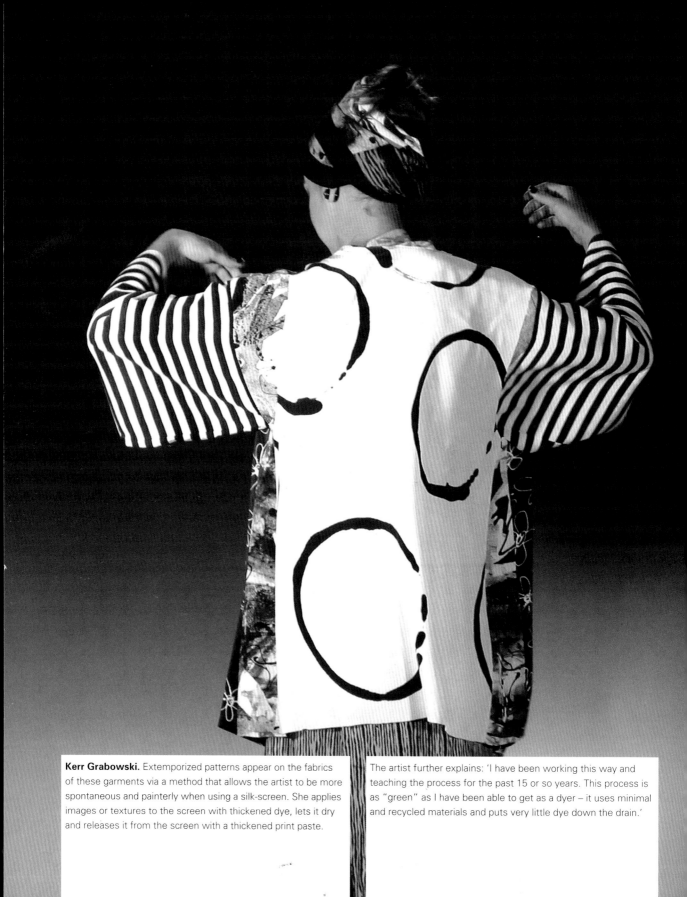

Kerr Grabowski. Extemporized patterns appear on the fabrics of these garments via a method that allows the artist to be more spontaneous and painterly when using a silk-screen. She applies images or textures to the screen with thickened dye, lets it dry and releases it from the screen with a thickened print paste.

The artist further explains: 'I have been working this way and teaching the process for the past 15 or so years. This process is as "green" as I have been able to get as a dyer – it uses minimal and recycled materials and puts very little dye down the drain.'

Afet Halil 50 x 50 cm (19.75 x 19.75 in). Research based on
the bangles worn by the Rabari tribe of northern India led this
artist to develop ideas based on the structure and quality of their
jewellery. This silk collar has been pleated and dyed before being
manipulated and sculpted around the chest area.

Ilkka Timonen for Virtuelli Design Studio 'Fall' 50 x 50 cm
(19.75 x 19.75 in). In a crisp graphic style reminiscent of some
of the wallpapers of the 1960s, this vibrant, digitally manipulated
textile design is a coordinating pattern for 'Black-Tree' (right) and
was based on the artist's own pictures of his blustery autumnal
Swedish environment.

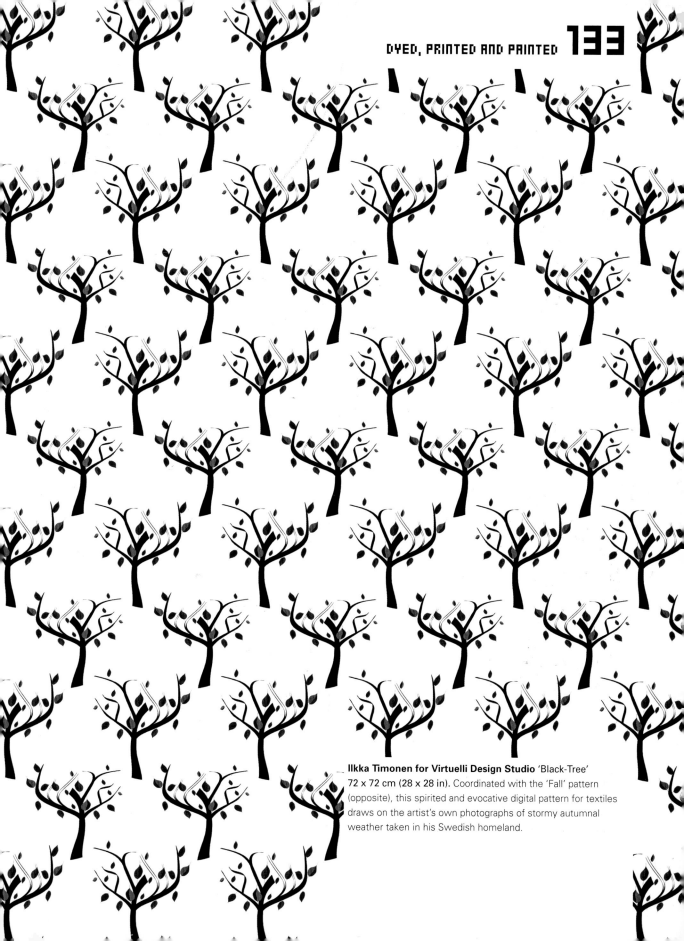

Ilkka Timonen for Virtuelli Design Studio 'Black-Tree'
72 x 72 cm (28 x 28 in). Coordinated with the 'Fall' pattern
(opposite), this spirited and evocative digital pattern for textiles
draws on the artist's own photographs of stormy autumnal
weather taken in his Swedish homeland.

Cressida Bell 'Design for Rug: Fishes' 180 x 130 cm (71 x 51 in). Stylized fishes swim in an orange and vermillion spotted sea in this hand painted gouache design for a large oval rug.

Laura Bissonnet 30 x 30 cm (12 x 12 in). Dyed and screen-printed fabrics in rich tones of rust and terracotta have been stitched together to form this unusually shaped bag.

Els van Baarle 90 x 180 cm (36 x 71 in). Splendidly coloured in deep red and mid blue, this abstract design on silk noil fabric has been screen-printed with thickened fibre-reactive dyes before being enhanced using batik techniques.

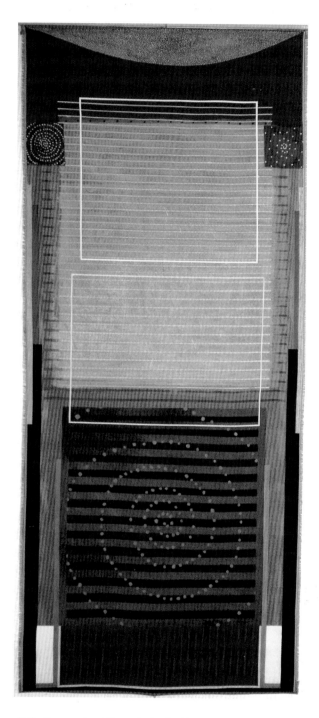

Sally Greaves-Lord Commission for Healix International
reception area 200 x 92 cm (78.75 x 36.25 in). Peripheral vision
is something that fascinates this artist. Fragments of other
patterns are envisaged as occurring simultaneously, but have not
yet been given form. The resulting multi-layered, hand painted
images have a profundity that engages the viewer on a deeper
level than the merely superficial.

Lorna Davis 'Chestnut' 109 x 107 cm (43 x 42 in). Isetta silk cotton and viscose silk satin have been dyed and discharge printed before being bonded together to produce this wall hanging inspired by a chestnut. The artist comments: 'I was able to create a new surface through the deconstruction of the yarns before bonding them with different fabric qualities. This allowed me to create the contrast of surfaces and colours that I gather from the organic matter I use for my inspiration.'

Helen Bolland 90 x 180 cm (36 x 71 in). The technique of
arashi shibori has allowed the valleys and peaks of this folded,
pleated, dyed and discharged scarf to be of different iridescent
colours. The artist comments: 'The majority of my work involves
the use of cylinders on which I wrap and bind the silk then
compress to create the pleats. The results of my work are
sometimes surprising, often joyously unpredictable, but always
personally rewarding.'

Mandy Southan 'Orange Tulips Blue Jug' 76 x 51 cm (30 x 20 in).
With its elegant composition and well-considered colouring, this
silk painting on *habotai* silk uses acid dyes and the *gutta* resist
technique in its production.

Arthur David 140 x 150 cm (55 x 59 in). Digitally transfer-printed onto polyester, this bold and sweeping design is intended to be used by couture and *à la mode* designers. The artist remarks: 'I work predominantly intuitively and experimentally, with drawing, painting and graphic design. Important sources of inspiration are the African cultures, the contemporary art scene and music.'

Arthur David 140 x 150 cm (55 x 59 in). After being digitally transfer-printed onto polyester, this unique shawl was hand cut to give it its individual appearance. The artist comments: 'I find the artistic ambivalences of the 1920s and 1930s interesting. Also interesting and/or eccentric humans can inspire me.'

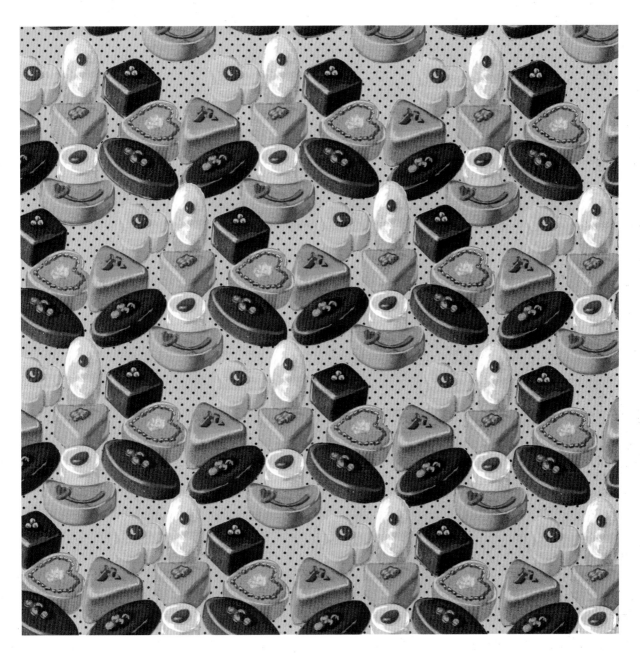

Danielle Budd 'Fondant Fancies' 50 x 50 cm (19.5 x 19.5 in).
Fondant fancies – which are small sugary confections – are the
unusual motifs on this sickly sweet digital fabric intended for
clutch bags and small accessories.

Dru Cole 'Cloud Scarves' 31 x 112 cm (12.25 x 44 in) each.
In these scarves, silk organza has been freely hand painted
with pigment crayons and dyes as a way of exploring colour
combinations and evoking particular moods.

Afet Halil 150 x 120 cm (59 x 47 in). Mysterious and sensual, this silk georgette piece was pleated, dyed and then draped to create an elaborate sleeve idea. The artist comments: 'My concept was to develop a collection of pieces that exaggerate and accentuate the female form.'

Dionne Yang 'White Shadow' 125 x 200 cm (49 x 78 in).
Inspired by shadows created by the trees in Hyde Park, London,
the artist has painted ink directly onto the photopositive to create
an atmospheric screen, before printing a piece of polyester
satin with a discharge paste. She continues: 'I like the idea of
accessorizing the fabric so that by adding bird brooches as a part
of the pattern the owner can play and interact with the fabric.'

Kerr Grabowski. Using a process the artist refers to as 'deconstructed' screen-printing, the prints on this silk *crêpe de Chine* reversible coat were achieved by painting dye paste onto a screen, allowing it to dry then releasing them onto the fabric with a clear sodium alginate emulsion.

Lorna Davis 35 x 93 cm (13.75 x 36.5 in). The naturally occurring texture of rust was explored and captured through drawing and photography to provide the stimulus for a foil and discharge-printed fabric sample.

Christina Strutt for Cabbages and Roses 'Indian Rose'
145 cm (57 in) wide. Evoking antique Indian wood block prints,
this linen and cotton mix fabric has been screen-printed in subtle
tones of grey and rose to create this precise impression.

Christina Strutt for Cabbages and Roses 'French Toile Raspberry' 145 cm (57 in) wide. Resplendent in raspberry pink, vintage fabrics inspired this monochromatic screen-printed design of carnations and stylized roses.

Kim Barnett for Birds in Skirts 'Red Tractor Cushion' 60 x 60 cm (23.5 x 23.5 in) **wide.** Tractors and pieces of machinery often feature in this designer's eclectic work. In this digital print they are combined with flowers to produce striking motifs.

Natasha Marshall 'The Park Collection' 137 cm (54 in) wide. Walking through the botanic gardens of Glasgow and Edinburgh, and the National Arboretum at Westonbirt, near Bath, inspired this artist's collection of designs.

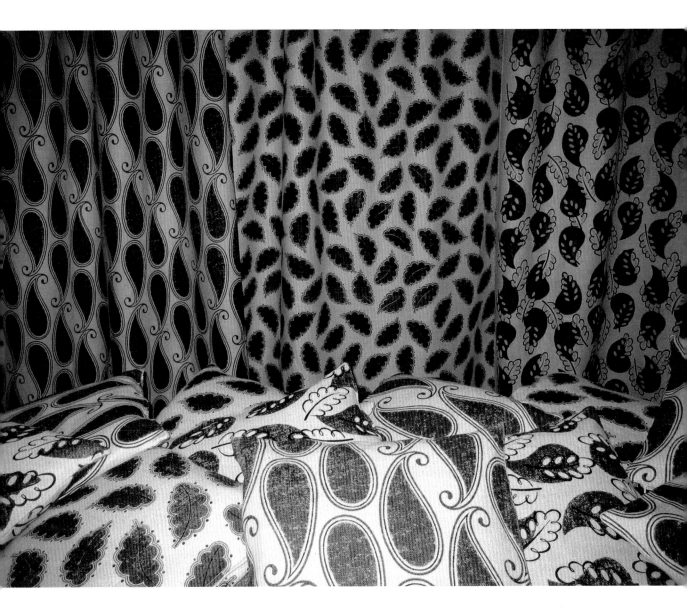

Cressida Bell 'Josephine' 140 cm (55 in) wide. This collection of linen fabrics for Borderline is screen-printed with a woodland leaf theme in deep madder red. The motifs have a slight 'sponged' effect, which softens them and enhances their resemblance to vintage hand-block prints.

Joanna Kinnersly-Taylor 'Jellies and Cutlery' 50 x 50 cm
(19.75 x 19.75 in) **each.** Jelly moulds, forks and spoons are
screen-printed in a regular, rhythmic composition to form the
culinary theme to this Irish table linen.

Timorous Beasties 136 cm (53.5 in) wide. Detailed graphic images of flowers and leaves appear in superb detail in this large-scale, screen-printed pattern on wool, which was created for use in interiors.

Brian Barratt 'Rose Stripe' 62 x 62 cm (24.5 x 24.5 in). Roses
are arguably the most popular of all flower motifs, and this artist
aimed to create his own take on the traditional floral repeat.
The intention was to mix a harder graphic style with the more
whimsical romantic floral. Vintage textiles with an injection of
1980's neon inspired his colour palette. The artist comments: 'I
believe floral designs represent many things to an individual and
I chose to include roses on the verge of decay, which is when I
believe they are most beautiful.'

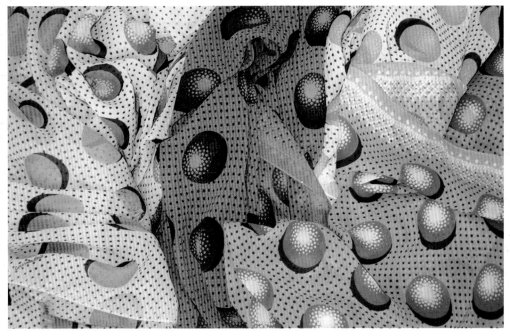

Cressida Bell 'Pinball' (above) 180 x 70 cm (71 x 27.5 in). The regular placing of a motif shaped like a pinball is the unusual design theme used to produce these splendid hand screen-printed silk georgette scarves. The evenly dotted background in the shadow colour of each design enhances the impression of movement and vitality as the fabric falls and drapes.

Rebecca Blackburn 'Derelict Site Cushion' (top) 29 x 54 cm (11.5 x 21 in). This artist has combined urban scenes, which she photographs and then screen-prints onto vintage floral fabrics, to achieve a homely, decorative feel. She continues: 'I feel I have combined two very diverse subject matters, which have strangely now formed a relationship to create aesthetically pleasing results.'

Carole Waller 'Wall Dress'. The result of a collaboration
between the artist and fashion designer Ray Harris, this semi-
transparent silk velvet dress features a pattern inspired by a
wall seen in the ancient lost city of Machu Picchu in Peru and
explores the duality of how clothes protect or reveal. The design
is drawn around the pattern pieces onto the fabric before it is cut
out and then hand painted using dyes. Once finished the cloth is
cut and constructed by a dressmaker.

Helen Bolland 'Dragon's Tail' 90 x 180 cm (36 x 71 in).
This 'Dragon's Tail' *shibori* scarf, inspired by peacock feathers,
is composed of many folds of fine silk in several coordinating
colours. The artist explains her technique: 'The silk is first
dyed a base colour. Then the scarf is dried and folded, and
wrapped around a stainless steel cylinder, bound with thread
and compressed to create the chevron pleating. Further dyeing
is then carried out before the cylinder is placed in a large pot of
steam to set the pleats.'

Isabella Whitworth 'Meadow' 20 x 135 cm (8 x 53 in). Layers
of overpainting using acid dyes and wax create a subtly toned
design that was based on studies of marshland.

Jason Black 51 x 41 cm (20 x 16 in). The underwater reefs and brilliantly coloured soft corals portrayed in this highly detailed silk painting are home to many diverse species of fish, including the angelfish and clownfish seen here.

Yun Ding 'Aqua Chameleon'. Forming part of this artist's final project for her MA in Design for Textiles Futures, this swimsuit uses photosensitive pigments, which react with the body's temperature, allowing the printed pattern to turn rapidly from a dark colour into bright pink and then back again when the surface temperatures fall.

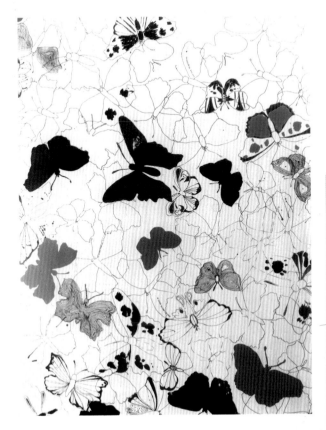

Zakee Shariff 'Butterflies Screen-print'. 119 cm x 84 cm
(47 x 33 in). Inspired by Michael Jackson's song 'Butterflies', this
screen print uses a limited palette and has a distinctly retro feel.

Timorous Beasties 136 cm (53.5 in). Drawing inspiration
from the silhouettes and coastlines of European countries, the
artist has created the shapes of a traditional damask weave.
The resulting motifs are also reminiscent of the psychoanalyst
Rorschach's famous ink blot images.

Isabella Whitworth 'Stalks' 20 x 135 cm (8 x 53 in). Drawings and observations of cultivated fields inspired this hand painted design on silk *crêpe de Chine*. The artist comments: 'This pattern relates to the regimented lines of stalks seen on the edge of a cultivated field, with the empty, unplanted spaces between.'

Sari Syväluoma 'Big Dolly' 60 x 60 cm (24 x 24 in). The clean lines of this screen-printed 100% linen cushion bridge the distance between 'Far North' and 'Exotic East'. The piece is rooted in the Scandinavian heritage of simplicity, combined with the bold colours and rich textures of the Indian subcontinent.

Jane Keith 'Hand Painted Essaoria Ties' 100 x 50 cm (36 x 19.5 in). This artist is best known for her hand painted silk ties, which are here shown after printing but before being separated. Ever-changing horizon lines, land and seascapes are her recurring inspirations and she uses them to create deceptively simple patterns and stripes.

Lidia Muro 'My Final Blue Little Dress' (top). Conceived as a moving sculpture, this piece of muslin fabric converted into a dress is covered randomly with irregular PVC printed triangles fused onto stiff fabric. The difference in rigidity and weight of the two materials allows the muslin and its triangles to fold obliquely and create diverse and unexpected shapes.

Mandy Southan 'Leaves after Rain' (above) 41 x 41 cm (16 x 16 in). In this highly accomplished and very beautiful silk painting, subtle tones and shades of purples, blues and mauves are set off perfectly by golden yellows. The artist comments: 'I set up my table in the garden following a rain shower and painted these *Fatsia japonica* leaves bejewelled by raindrops. The shapes of the leaves are true to nature but the colours are mine!'

Dionne Yang 'Blue' 35 x 35 cm (13.75 x 13.75 in). Created with childrens' wear in mind, this digitally-printed silk satin of imaginary birds and creatures has a coordinating range of printed cushions and dolls, to suggest that the two-dimensional patterns pop out of the fabric and transform into three-dimensional items.

India Flint '*Prunus* ecoprint' 90 x 90 cm (36 x 36 in). As a result of her explorations and research into natural dyes, this Australian artist has developed a process she terms an 'ecoprint', which is an ecologically sustainable, plant-based printing process giving brilliant colour to cloth. Shown here is a leaf print on silk satin.

Satu Makkonen for Hau Hauz 'Tango Purple' 25 x 30 cm (10 x 12 in). This purse, which is hand screen-printed onto radiant purple linen, is made by a Finnish company that specializes in strong colour combinations and large prints.

Jane Keith 'Blue Medina' 130 x 130 cm (51 x 51 in). Multicoloured vertical stripes break up the rich blues in this hand printed and painted wall hanging, inspired by the vibrant images and colours of Morocco.

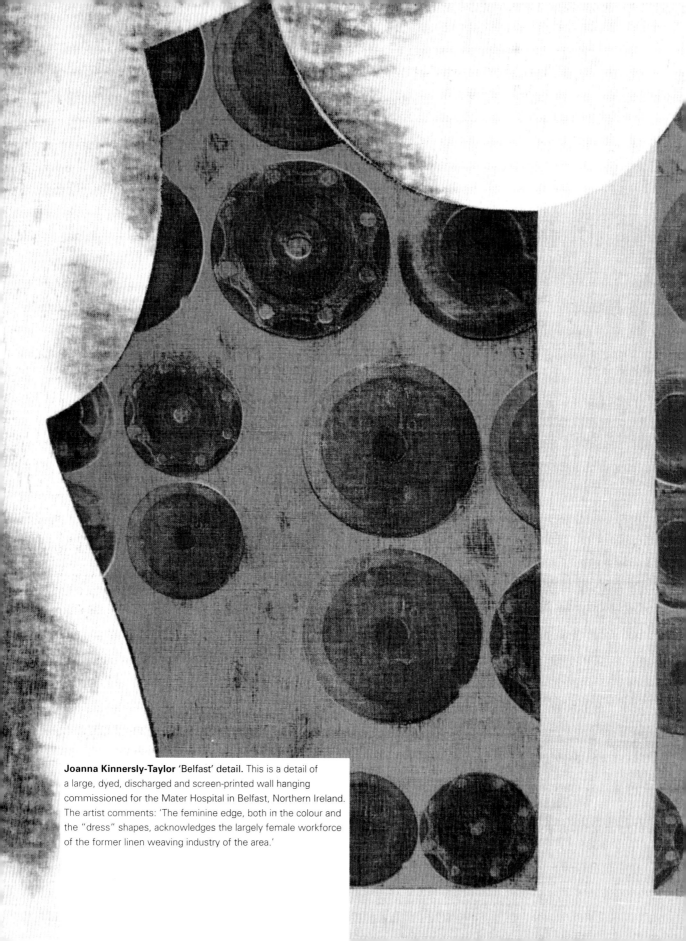

Joanna Kinnersly-Taylor 'Belfast' detail. This is a detail of a large, dyed, discharged and screen-printed wall hanging commissioned for the Mater Hospital in Belfast, Northern Ireland. The artist comments: 'The feminine edge, both in the colour and the "dress" shapes, acknowledges the largely female workforce of the former linen weaving industry of the area.'

Saori Okabe in collaboration with Elena Tsyptakova
96 x 63 cm (37.75 x 25 in). Line drawings derived from the flowers of tree peonies are overprinted using flock paste onto dip-dyed mauve cashmere, which gives this fabric sample a sumptuous quality.

Mandy Southan 'Morning Tulips' 48 x 57 cm (19 x 22.5 in).
Almost three-dimensional, these blossoms stand out against
their shadowy blue-toned background. The artist comments:
'I think silk painting is the best medium for capturing the pure
colours of flowers and the delicate sheen of their petals. A few
favourite flowers entice me back again and again. Tulips are
one of these seductive goddesses. I love their gorgeous glossy
blooms and curling leaves.'

Dionne Yang 'Hanbok Garment'. These garments are a redesigned version of the traditional Korean upper wear *hanbok-jeogory*. The artist comments: 'Made with my own digitally printed fabric, the *jeogory* represents my rooted Korean identity; one that would never be changed however big the influence might be, whilst the ruffles, silk and printed patterns represent my multicultural experiences. Traditionally, the *jeogory* is worn like a bolero, but I decided only to make the upper garment to represent and express the feeling of vulnerability I occasionally felt as a foreigner living in London. I could not help but become unnecessarily overly conscious of myself, feeling awkward, vulnerable and half-naked, time after time.'

Betsy Sterling Benjamin 'Blue Lotus of Lumbini'
108 x 78 cm (42.5 x 30.75 in). This delicately coloured and
evocative silk wall hanging was named after the Lumbini Garden,
where the Buddha was born, and was created via the process
of *rozome*. The subtly shaded colouring is the result of a highly
skilled technique, which uses custom-made round Japanese
brushes to apply and blend the colour evenly from transparent
to saturated, allowing for wonderful luminous effects.

Kerr Grabowski 'Deconstructed' 68 x 101 cm (26.75 x
39.75 in). Using fibre-reactive dye on silk *crêpe de Chine*,
this 'Deconstructed' screen-print gives a unique distressed
appearance to the fabric because of its array of disintegrating
colours and haphazard textures.

Dorothy Bunny Bowen 'Glencoe, Scotland' 56 x 71 cm
(22 x 28 in). Austere and powerful, this *rozome* on silk study
of Glencoe in Scotland invokes strong feelings. The artist
comments: 'My earliest memories are of the soft blue mountains
that encircle the hillside home of my childhood. Once a man
bought one of my batiks because it reminded him of Glencoe,
Scotland, and I vowed to someday see that place. When finally
I was able to go, I found that Glencoe is indeed wild, empty and
fiercely beautiful.'

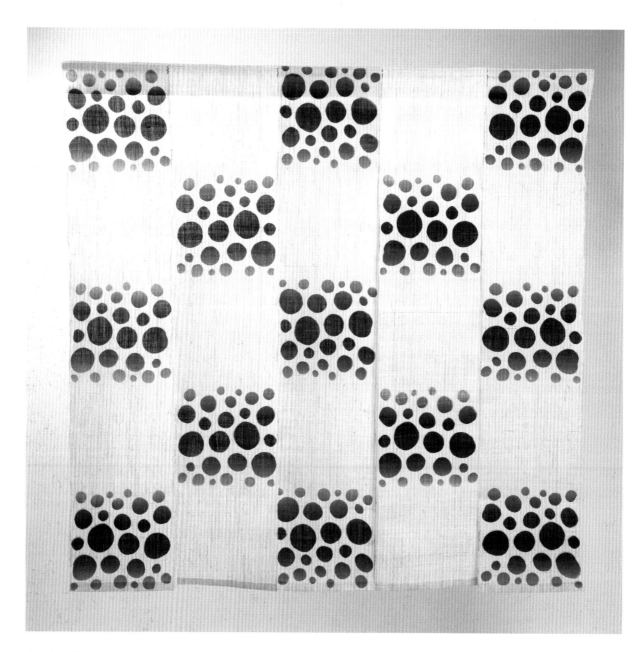

Rowland Ricketts 150 x 150 cm (59 x 59 in). This hemp fabric partition was created using natural indigo, which the artist grew and processed himself, and the paste-resist technique of *katazome*. The artist explains: 'My decision to work this way is one that consciously favours slower, natural processes and materials. I am aware of a connection that leads not just from my teachers to me, but one that reaches back to my teacher's teachers, back into a past through the accumulated experiences of all who have ever worked with this unique dye.'

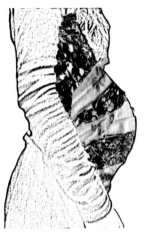

Marion Piffaut 'Pregnant' (top) 60 x 20 cm (24 x 8 in). Within the pleats in this top for a pregnant woman lies a surprise. There is one pattern visible on the fabric and another pattern hidden inside the pleats. The artist explains: 'I pleated my fabric with a heat press and printed it with transfer ink to use less water, to make my process cleaner. There is a plastic sheet bonded to the pleats. The pleats open when the plastic sheet peels off over time, when you wear or wash the clothes.'

Laura-Jane O'Kane (above) 90 cm (35.5 in) wide. Featuring typically Spanish motifs such as a flamenco dancer, a matador and a bull, this is a detail from a hand screen-printed and -painted silk fabric created as part of the artist's final year college project.

Arthur David 140 x 150 cm (55 x 59 in). Stylish and bold, this digitally manipulated textile design is an amalgam of graphic design, drawing and painting, and is intended for couture and *à la mode* designers. The artist remarks: 'I work predominantly intuitively and experimentally, with drawing, painting and graphic design. Important sources of inspiration are the African cultures, the contemporary art scene and music.'

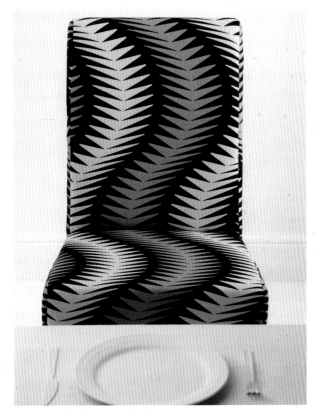

Natasha Marshall 'The Park Collection' 137 cm (54 in) wide. Zigzags in blue, navy and white curve up and down this chair, upholstered in a cotton and linen fabric. It has a definite 1920s influence, with its enlarged details and strong lines, together with curving arabesques and bold colour combinations.

Satu Makkomen for Hau Hauz 25 x 30 cm (10 x 12 in). A simple black line pattern is hand screen-printed onto 100% white linen, to produce an elegant fashion accessory for this Finnish design company.

Lorna Davis 40 x 79 cm (16 x 31 in). The artist has applied crimp paste to this dyed and printed experimental fabric sample and left it in place for 48 hours in order to radically alter the surface texture of the fabric.

Suzanne Silk 'Crane Kimono'. An art form in itself, the kimono is a superb canvas for creative designs. Here, the designer has used multi-layered silk organza which has been adorned using myriad techniques to produce a unique garment.

Design Team Nya Nordiska 'Carmen' 330 cm (130 in) wide. Delicately machine embroidered in a graphic leaf pattern, this sheer polyester organza fabric has a romantic and sensuous charm.

Carole Waller 'Adjustment'. Letters and parts of words half seen lend an air of inscrutability and an offbeat message to this hand painted dress. The artist comments: The Adjustment series was made just after 9/11 – when making a collection of painted clothes seemed an irrelevant thing to be doing after such an event.'

Kerr Grabowski. Dots dripped onto a screen form intriguing, nebulous shapes in this example of deconstructed screen-printing. The artist comments: 'This is one of my favourite fabrics – the purity of the marks speaks to me and I love the fact that you can achieve these beautiful, subtle marks with such minimal materials.'

Timorous Beasties 'Lace Thistle' 150 cm (59 in) wide. Thistles form a prickly motif for this screen printed voile. The designer comments: 'The subtlety of the graphic-printed organic forms demonstrates the unique qualities that can be produced through hand printing.'

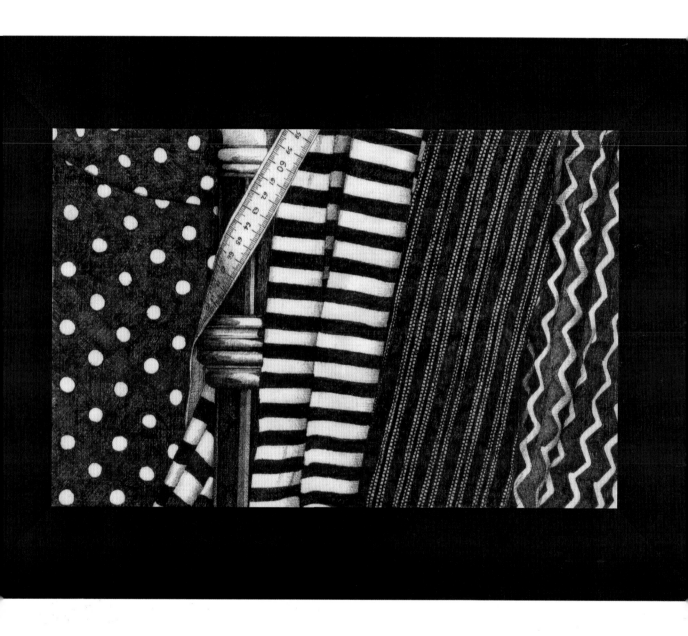

Paddy Killer 'My Bedpost Overnight' 34 x 46 cm (13.5 x 18 in). Polka dots, stripes, zigzags and a tape measure are captured with astonishing accuracy in this drawing in Indian ink on silk. The artist comments on her 'Eureka!' moment: 'I woke up and thought, "What a great composition!", so I took a digital image at the bottom of my bed. I made an outline drawing onto silk with my technical pen and then bonded the silk onto mounting card before framing it.'

Paddy Killer 'Textile Study with Moth' 39 x 30 cm (15 x 12 in).
Highly skilled drawing is the main basis for this artist's work and
she draws her detailed pictures directly onto silk using a technical
pen and black Indian ink. The content of this piece reflects the
artist's continuing investigations. She says: 'Researching is
all-important to me, and I see my work as a constant discovery,
whether it is learning a new computer program, or the
symbolism found in the art of a bygone world.'

Kerr Grabowski 98 x 80 cm (38.5 x 31.5 in). Created by placing torn newspaper on the fabric as a stencil and then screen-printing, this print is from an ongoing series based around the artist's grandparents and their tempestuous marriage and life. The artist comments: 'This is pretty much a "stream of consciousness" piece, as I do not do sketches beforehand, preferring to draw back into the prints.'

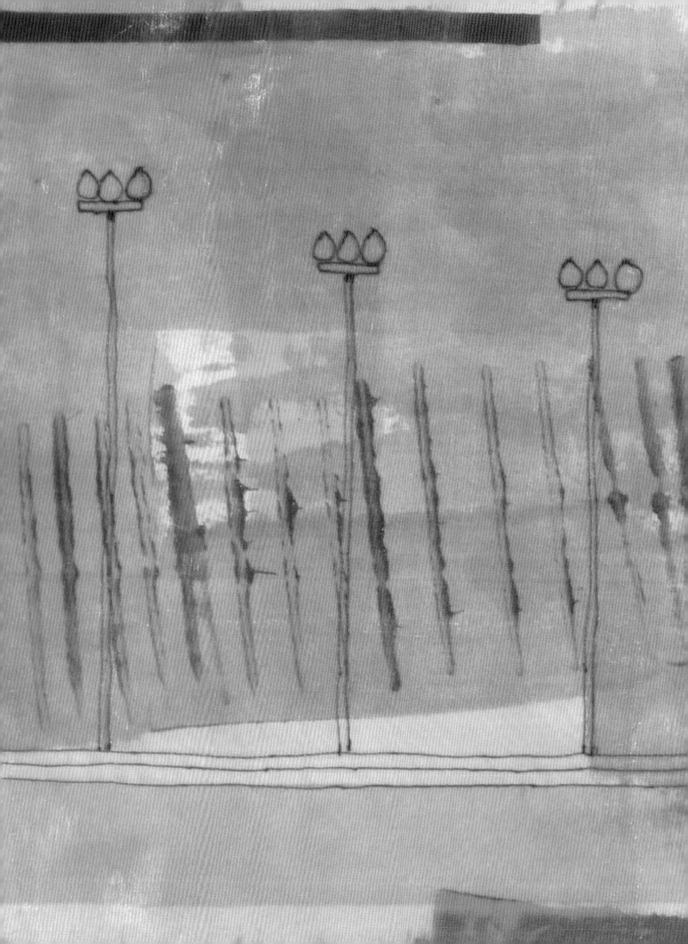

MIXED MEDIA AND STITCHED TEXTILES

The majority of the textiles in this section have been created using more than one technique. The artists' methods include stitching and embroidery – by hand or machine, felting, dyeing, appliqué, quilting, needle punching and digital- and screen-printing. The items produced range from garments and accessories to decorative items for the home as well as a number of art pieces.

Many of the featured artists like to experiment with different methods and materials in order to capture or evoke a particular feeling or atmosphere. The desire to tell a story or convey humour is often a strongly motivating force; several of these pieces are pictorial illustrations that recount a personal anecdote, present a narrative, or even retell traditional tales.

Many of these designs are influenced by a variety of cultural and historical factors, from Art Nouveau prints and antique embroidery samplers to architectural design, mythology and folklore, and interpret these in new and imaginative ways. There are also examples of mixed-media textiles that use unusual and distinctive materials such as beads, foil and shells, including the work of one innovative designer who has incorporated hand-embroidered organic photovoltaic cells, computerized circuit-board designs and conductive-thread hand embroidery for circuitry in her pieces!

Betsy Sterling Benjamin in collaboration with Luanne Rimel
'Door to the Sea' 198 x 74 cm (78 x 29 in). Conceived as a visual
meditation, this large hand painted *rozome* silk wall hanging is
a reflective image of the main gate of the temple of Honen-in,
Japan. It has been positioned under a digitally-printed image
of the sea that contains a machine-embroidered text excerpt
penned by the Chilean poet Pablo Neruda.

Carol Naylor 'Early Morning' 20 x 28 cm (8 x 11 in). In this densely stitched machine embroidery, swathes of colour in a range of lavender, blue and gold threads explore the effect of early morning light on the landscape.

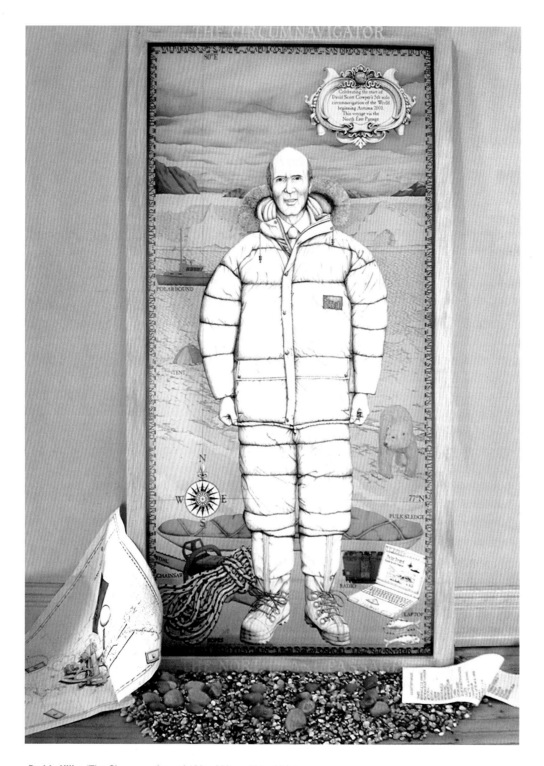

Paddy Killer 'The Circumnavigator' 130 x 250 cm (51 x 98 in).
Celebrating the artist's friend, yachtsman David Scott Cowper,
who began his fifth solo circumnavigation of the world in 2002,
this portrait has been hand drawn onto opaque silk and appliquéd
onto silk organza. Details such as a polar bear and an ice floe
were subsequently included, before adding some areas of free-
machined vermicelli embroidery.

Laura McCafferty 'At the Line' 85 x 65 cm (34 x 25.5 in).
Hanging the washing out is the domestic activity portrayed in this
screen-printed and appliquéd textile. The artist comments: 'This
was one of the first pieces that I completed after graduating. I
turned to my family for inspiration and I captured my Nana in my
Auntie's garden. I like the plants growing up along the bottom
– it gives the impression of peering in on her. I used a lot of old
fabrics on this one – pillow cases and old clothes.'

Helen Melvin 'Sea and Sand' 80 x 100 cm (31.25 x 36 in).
Many fibres and fabrics were dyed using natural dyes such as
madder and weld, then were layered, felted and machine-stitched
together to produce this evocative wall hanging. The artist explains:
'This is part of a series I produced in response to a childhood
memory of the sea encroaching on the sand. In each picture, the
sea has become more violent and the waves have gone from
curling onto the beach to crashing down with violence.'

Helen Melvin 'Rough Sea' 44 x 83 cm (17.25 x 32.5 in). Inspired
by the natural beauty of the British coastline, this artist's natural
dyed, felted and machine-stitched wall hanging reflects her own
internal vision, as well as a love of the environment and a sense
of it descending into chaos.

Naomi Renouf 'Stones, Sea, Sand' 39 x 66 cm (15.25 x 26 in).
Inspired by the coast off the Channel Island of Jersey during the
summer, this piece has been machine-stitched and free-machine
embroidered with a variety of fabrics, beads and shells.

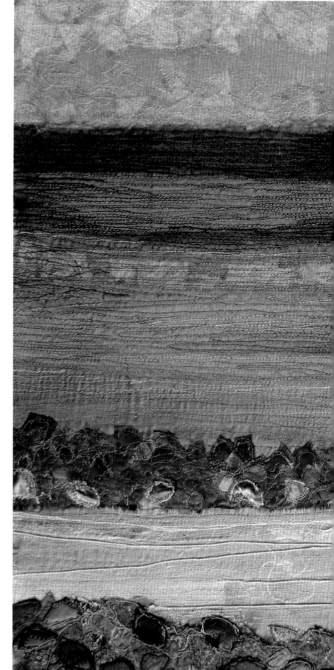

Karen Stiehl Osborn 'Fragments' 30 x 30 cm (12 x 12 in). This quilt, which incorporates images of fragments of buildings and letters, has been dyed, stitched and screen-printed in shades and tones of blue and mauve.

Naomi Renouf 'Archirondel'. Archirondel is the name of a beach in Jersey, the largest of the Channel Islands situated between England and France, and was the inspiration for this piece created with layered voile and other fabrics stitched together using free machine embroidery.

Alicia Merrett 'Syncopation' 95 x 169 cm (37.5 x 66.5 cm).
This striped quilt uses fabrics hand dyed by Heidi Stoll-Weber.
Jazz and ragtime music were the inspiration, hence the recurring
keyboard motif. The artist comments: 'This contemporary design
is an attempt to transpose the musical effect of the syncopated
beat onto the visual field.'

Helen Suzanne Alexander 'Silver Birch' detail 35 x 29 cm
(13.75 x 11.5 in). Giving a wonderful optical illusion of wood
grain underneath peeling bark, the handmade woollen felt for
this piece is mounted on a double layer of two-tone organza. The
artist explains: 'Successive layers of threads and heat dissolving
fabric were applied with needle felting, and then burned back
before the next layer was added. There is no stitching to this
piece apart from the few surface embroidered lines to indicate
horizontal marks in the bark.'

Naomi Renouf 'Cherry Blossom' 43 x 43 cm (17 x 17 in). A cherry tree in full blossom is the subject of this evocative, free-machine embroidered fabric assemblage.

Tilleke Schwarz 'What You See is What You Get' 75 x 67 cm (29.5 x 26 in). Containing texts from contemporary conversations, this textile piece on hand dyed blue linen has a striking central feature of long silk threads, resembling a waterfall with flowers beneath. Folk art, cats and daily life are sources of inspiration for the artist. She comments on her work: 'The viewer may assemble the stories to produce chronological and causal structures. Actually, the viewer might step into the role of the "author". It can become a kind of play between the viewer and me. The work also relates to the history of humanity that is determined through stories. The humour in my work is typical for my Jewish background: a mixture of a laugh and a tear.'

Karen Stiehl Osborn 'Tropical Blues' 51 x 38 cm (20 x 15 in).
The artist was inspired by the cool waters, luscious greenery and
bright splashes of colour found in the Caribbean to produce this
evocative quilt, which has been dyed, printed and stitched.

Clare Lane 'The Palm House' 97 x 79 cm (38 x 31 in). Colour, place and perception of space are the principal elements of this artist's digitally-printed, stitched and embellished textile work. She continues: 'My visual interest is in the portrayal of the built environment as the landscape of a modern urban society, its changing spaces and places, and its cyclical regeneration.'

Lois Woodger 'Orford Hanging' 140 x 39 cm (55 x 15.25 in). A combination of digital photography, paint and stitching creates this evocative wall hanging based on aspects of the tiny village of Orford on the east coast of England. The artist comments: 'I use a combination of media in my work – photography, to capture the sights that inspire me, painting, to interpret what I see, and stitching. My work reflects my love of the seashore.'

Kate Hyde. Layered and stitched, this experimental piece encompasses many techniques. The artist comments: 'While studying embroidery I was encouraged to learn a range of skills: layering materials, stitching, folding, cutting, ripping and applying colour through various print and dye techniques. I see the mediums as being intertwined, bridging the gap between drawn and painted art, and fashion; works to be seen equally as exhibition pieces and as wearable garments.'

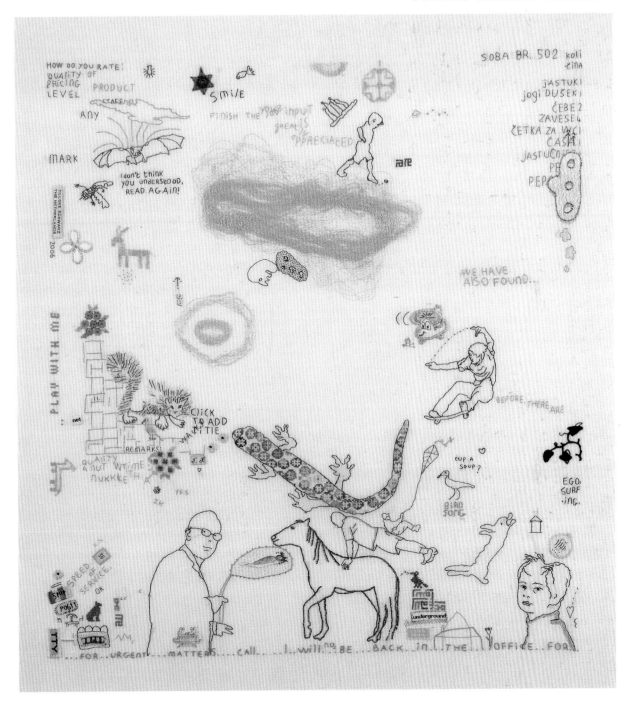

Tilleke Schwarz 'Play with Me' 71 x 65 cm (28 x 25.5 in).
Composed of a number of seemingly unrelated images, which were mostly taken from daily newspapers, these graphic pictures strategically stitched onto linen cloth use all manner of threads, scraps of fabrics, lace and a very special Japanese green metallic thread in their depiction. The artist comments: 'My work can be understood as a kind of visual poetry. It is a mixture of contemporary influences, graffiti, icons, texts and images from traditional samplers. The work contains narrative elements, not really complete stories with a beginning, a storyline, and an end. On the contrary, the narrative structures are used as a form of communication with the viewer. The viewer is invited to decipher connections or to create them.'

Carol Naylor 'Under Italian Sky' 20 x 26 cm (8 x 10.25 in).
Cypress trees and poppies in cornfields seen on visits to Italy
have inspired this machine embroidery, which uses viscose,
metallic, woollen and cotton threads. The artist comments: 'This
is a response to the land rather than an attempt to imitate reality.'

Ingrid Tait for Tait & Style 'Green Braw Birdie' 26 x 26 cm (10.25 x 10.25 in). This is a fun creation from a small company whose staff live and work in the Orkney Islands, Scotland. The designers comment: 'We've been creating knitted creatures for a few years now and the bird "grew" from there; it also led to a scarf design. It starts life in the workshop, where the lambswool fabric is made in large sheets using the knitting machines; all this fabric is then felted. They then get passed onto our team of local outworkers who make up the main body of the birds and then decorate them with embroidery and buttons.'

Susan Taber Avila 'Disco Fever' 107 x 125 x 3.5 cm (42 x 49 x 1.5 in). Using digitally-printed cotton and industrial felt, this machine-stitched quilt pays homage to the late Gaza Bowen, an artist famous for making incredible shoes, both as art objects and as wearable items. The artist continues: 'The gold beaded platform sandal pictured in the centre of the piece belonged to Gaza. The text, which is discharged from the digitally-printed fabric, reminds us of the 1970s dance craze that made a global impact. Stitching covers the piece as embellishment but also as a veil of memory.'

Clare Lane 'Ancoats' 97 x 79 cm (38 x 31 in). A scene of urban decay is recreated via drawing, painting and photographing images, which are then transferred to a computer where they are layered and digitally manipulated. The final process of stitching texture and line back into a piece brings out a three-dimensional quality, an echo of the source.

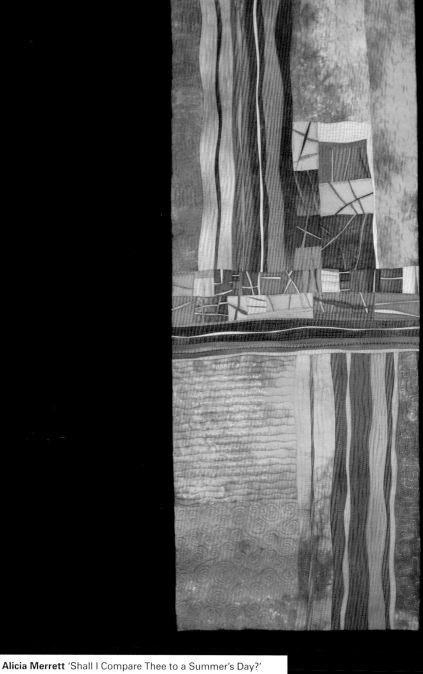

Alicia Merrett 'Shall I Compare Thee to a Summer's Day?'
46 x 122 cm (18 x 48 in). Inspired by Shakespeare's Sonnet
Number 18, this contemporary textile is composed of pieces
of fabric that have been hand dyed by Heidi Stoll Weber. The
artwork is based on the patchwork and quilting tradition but with
technical variations, being layered with wadding and backing
before being machine stitched.

Susan Taber Avila 'Garden Party' 19 x 40.5 x 40.5 cm (7.5 x 16 x 16 in). Stitched shoes are the subject of this extraordinary textile art piece that plays on the history of shoes as fetishist or fantasy objects, especially the urban myth of drinking champagne out of a slipper. The work can be manually rotated, implying that a tame party could spin out of control. Digital photographs of grass or lawn form the skins of the shoes, while industrial felt and red fabric remnants add structure to the form that is entirely stitched by the artist.

Poppy Treffry 23 x 19 cm (9 x 7.5 in). This jolly handbag was inspired by summers spent on the Isles of Scilly where old-fashioned open tractors are still used for almost all agricultural pursuits, for transport and as fire engines. The piece features appliquéd vintage fabrics and freehand machine embroidery on heavy red cotton drill with a ticking lining.

Alison Willoughby. Worn as a garment or displayed in a glass case on the wall, this skirt is the result of a long process of research based on the alleys and passageways of the inner city. The artist records suitable images through photography, amassing hundreds of stills to dissect and then translate into fabric samples, which are then worded in a variety of materials.

Barbara Fidoe 'What Have They Done?' 26 x 240 cm (10.25 x 94.5 in). Layering techniques applied to a cotton base cloth replicate the look of devoré velvet in this chartreuse and turquoise piece. Hand screen-printing and embroidery have been added to enhance the piece.

Tiziana Tateo 'Leopold' 68 x 51 cm (26.75 x 20 in). This striking portrait of a young man has been accomplished by a comprehensive mixed media technique that uses tissue paper, painted cotton and nappy (diaper) liner which are painted and transferred onto calico and machine embroidered on tulle using water-soluble paper.

Joan Schultz 'Farmers Market 28 Views' 122 x 122 cm (48 x 48 in). 28 photocopied images have been transferred onto paper and silk packets and laminated onto one piece of heavy silk to make this quilt. At the top and bottom appear silk-painted water pieces, giving the whole piece an intriguing rain soaked look.

Joan Schulze 'City Tempo' 109 x 109 cm (43 x 43 in). This quilt on a quilt features mark making that resembles calligraphy. The artist explains: 'The large quilted piece is monoprinted and machine quilted. The central panels are glue-transferred and layered pieces, machine quilted and finished with an edge. This is attached to the larger quilt using Velcro. Each part can visually function by itself as a unique work … I like the way they work together.'

Naomi Renouf 'Laburnum Tree' 43 x 43 cm (17 x 17 in).
Evoking springtime with its golden yellow blossoms, this portrait
of a laburnum tree is machine embroidered, layered with voile
and appliquéd with a plethora of different textured fabrics.

Elena Corchero 'Graphic Necklace' 36 x 20 cm (14 x 8 in).
Project sponsored by 'Distance Lab'; www.distancelab.org
Special thanks to Crispin Jones's collaboration for electronics;
www.mr-jones.org. Rather surprisingly, the intricate images
of birds and abstract swirls in this necklace contain hand
embroidered organic photovoltaic cells, computerized circuit
board designs and conductive-thread hand embroidery for
circuitry. These allow the necklace to charge during the day
and to shine gently at night.

Kelly Woollard 'In Time' 50 x 45 cm (19.75 x 18 in). Vintage
damask fabric and calico are pierced and layered in a design
inspired by an eighteenth-century design, to produce this unique
textile wall clock.

Tiziana Tateo 'Lunia' (top) 49 x 52 cm (19 x 20.5 in). A painting by the artist Amedeo Modigliani was the inspiration for a portrait realized in textiles by this mixed-media artist. The artist combined marks and stitches on tissue paper, embossed copper metal, hand painted velvet and dyed cotton net and machine-embroidered tulle using water-soluble paper.

Jenni Cadman 'Dandelion Clocks' (above) 81 x 50 cm (32 x 19.75 in). In this wall hanging, delicate rusted lines interspersed by line images, themselves inspired by dandelions, appear so distressed that they resemble an ancient Egyptian hieroglyph.

Elana Herzog 100 x 50 cm (39.25 x 19.75 in). Untitled piece from 'Civilization and its Discontents'. Carpet and tapestry are a widespread form of material culture, whose uses range from providing comfort and symbolizing wealth to telling stories. The artist explains that this project 'reflects an ongoing fascination with carpets as vehicles of cultural narratives and motifs, and as an indicator of trends in design, taste and technology'.

Nadia Sparham 'Curly Tree Tweed Cushion' 40 x 40 cm (16 x 16 in). Referencing Gustav Klimt and others of the Vienna Succession movement, the swirling patterns on this cushion have been appliquéd and embroidered by hand and machine.

Tilleke Schwarz '100% Checked' 67 x 60 cm (26 x 24 in).
Exploring the topic of 'security', this stitched mixed media piece on dyed linen contains many references to its theme. The artist explains: '"100% Checked" is about security. The title was machine stitched. Therefore, it will be like a foreign item that does not really belong. Similar to when you pass through security at the airport and no matter how beautiful your suitcase looks; you get a security tag on it. Underneath the title is a quote from a person who felt chased and controlled everywhere she went. Security measurements have a great influence on our lives and make us behave more strangely than ever.'

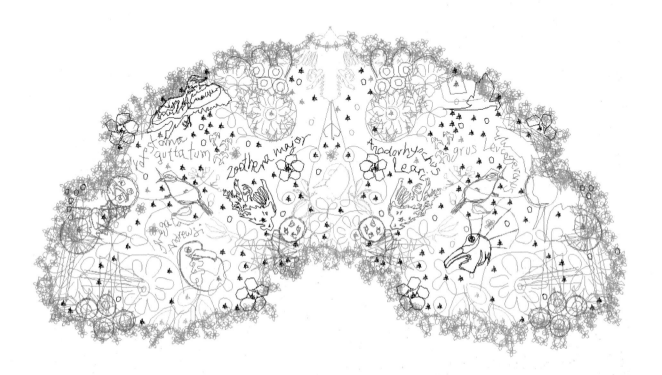

Elena Corchero 'Graphic Fan Lace' 38 x 8 cm (15 x 3 in).
Project sponsored by 'Distance Lab'; www.distancelab.org
Special thanks to Crispin Jones's collaboration for electronics;
www.mr-jones.org. This hand-held embroidered and
embellished fan stores solar power during the day, ready to be
transformed into an ornamental light display for the home at
night by incorporating solar cells into the textile's fabric.

Arlé Sklar-Weinstein 'Finding Myself in Santa Fe' 197 x
140 cm (77.5 x 55 in). This artist creates elaborate fabric
constructions that address physical geography, cultural influences
and interior self-awareness. She describes this work as 'made
up of three distinct layers: the base is a digital image transfer of
a skyscape, photographed while travelling from Boulder to Sante
Fe; at the bottom is a Santa Domingo bird symbol; near the top is
a blue sphere image which I use in my work as a symbol of my
higher self'.

Donatella Crippa 'Peter and the Wolf' 37 x 28 cm (14.5 x 11 in).
Prokofiev's famous composition of 'Peter and the Wolf' was
the inspiration for this engaging textile illustration. The author
felt it was appropriate to give this piece a rustic Russian feel, so
she used old oriental upholstery fabric for Peter's trousers and
soft checked leather for his boots. She comments: 'I decided
to illustrate the moment when Peter catches the naughty wolf
that has eaten his precious friend, Sonja the duck! Although
the story is set in the bitterly cold Russian winter, I wanted the
sun to shine for Peter. So I created a big sun using a discharge
technique. Sasha the bird, the felted wolf and some vintage lace
leaves complete the fabric collage.'

Arlé Sklar-Weinstein 'Metro Textural 2: The Gates' 91 x 91 cm
(36 x 36 in). Taking inspiration from Christo's and Jean-Claude's
'Gates' installation in Central Park, New York, in 2005, this fabric
assemblage incorporates several samples of the actual gate
fabric, an orange woven plastic-like composition that contrasts
sharply with the white sky and dark sculptural trees.

Donatella Crippa 'Soffiasbuffa' 33 x 30 cm (13 x 12 in).
Part of a project called 'Voices of African Tam-tam', this is an
appliquéd textile illustration of a story from Botswana, entitled
'Soffiasbuffa'. To create this image the artist used plain cottons
and pieces of handmade felt that she dyed in order to achieve a
colour range that reminded her of the plains of Africa. The artist
goes on to say: 'The baobab tree leaves have been created by
brushing hot wax onto thick cotton, then painting them with
liquid dyes. The hair of both children has been done with machine
embroidery and I have used real beads for the necklace.'

Alice Kettle 'Odyssey' detail 180 x 385 cm (71 x 151.5 in).
Powerful and beautiful, this large and dense machine embroidery
portrays people and objects – both recognizable and unknown
– and creates an impressive sweep of colour and imagery.

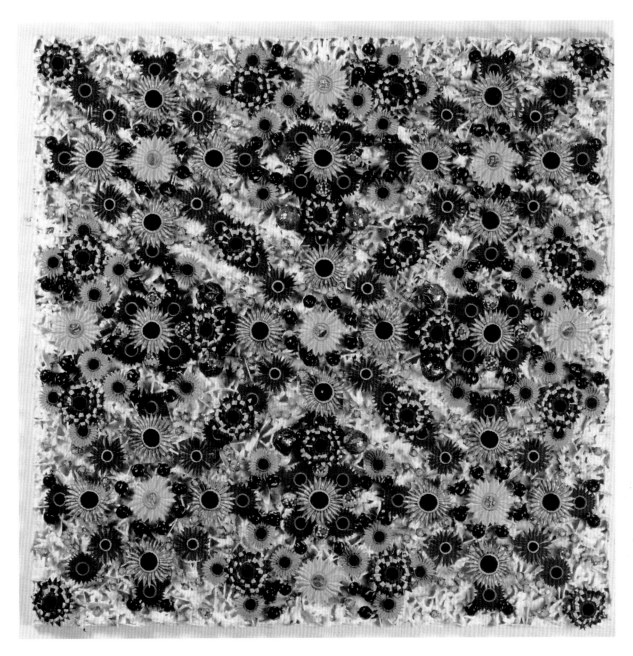

Michael Brennand-Wood 90 x 90 x 7 cm (35.5 x 35.5 x 2.75 in).
Inspired by traditions of floral imagery, this artist has combined
computerized machine embroidery, acrylic paint, wood, glass and
collage. The work is colourful, dramatic, rhythmic and holographic
in feeling, with intense detail that merges at a distance into an
optical configuration.

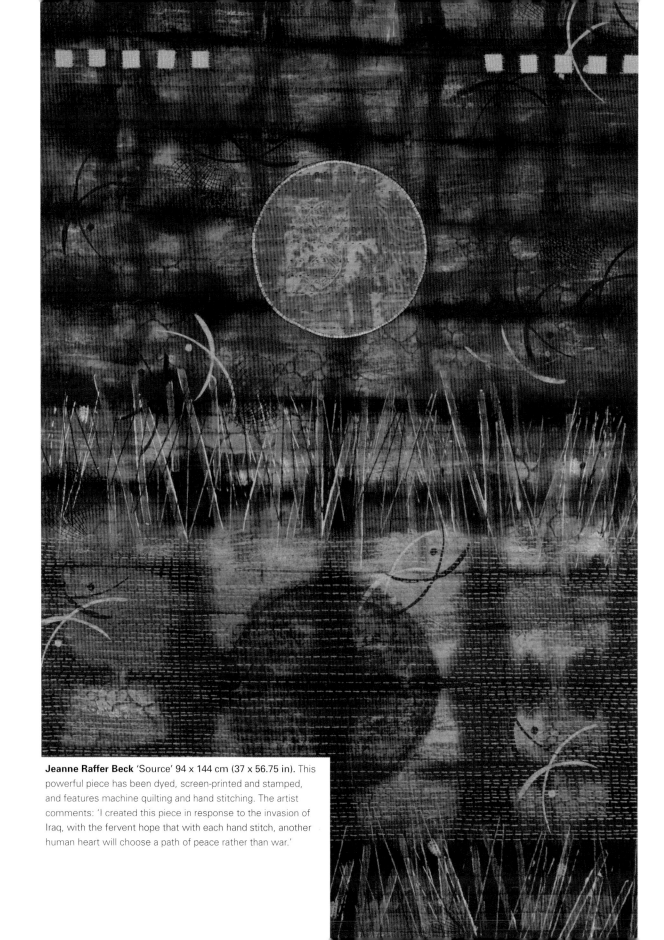

Jeanne Raffer Beck 'Source' 94 x 144 cm (37 x 56.75 in). This powerful piece has been dyed, screen-printed and stamped, and features machine quilting and hand stitching. The artist comments: 'I created this piece in response to the invasion of Iraq, with the fervent hope that with each hand stitch, another human heart will choose a path of peace rather than war.'

Donatella Crippa 'It Keeps You Running' (top) 33 x 27 cm (13 x 10.5 in). Brightly coloured fields in reds and pinks are set against a mustard yellow sky in this appliquéd textile illustration of a woman running after her chickens. Small creatures resembling tortoises are placed in the foreground to counteract the speed of the running birds on higher grounds.

Poppy Treffry 'I Love Tea' detail (above). Earl Grey is a delicious blended tea originally based on China tea, with the addition of a little bergamot oil. It is the subject of this piece from the artist's collection of appliquéd and free-machine embroidered tea and coffee themed items.

Charlotte Yde 'Bloody Garden' 111 x 132 cm (43.75 x 60 in).
Containing both natural and mythological images and symbols,
this blood-red, black and green striped quilted piece is full of
unusual details that seem both primeval and contemporary.

Nadia Sparham 'Banimal Cushion' 30 x 40 cm (12 x 16 in).
Looking like a creature from the animated film *The Yellow Submarine*, the appliquéd and embroidered 'Banimal' on this cushion is, in fact, a figment of the artist's fertile imagination.

Nadia Sparham 'Sun Tree Cushion' 30 x 40 cm (12 x 16 in).
A big orange sun shape dominates this stitched and appliquéd cushion with additional freehand machine embroidery. The cushion takes its inspiration from ancient Chinese pottery.

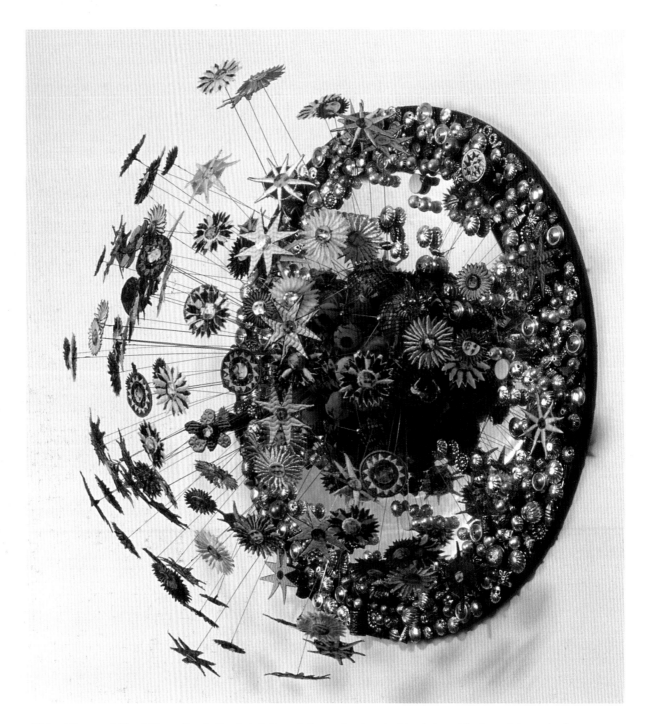

Michael Brennand-Wood 'Flower Head – Narcissistic Butterfly'
60 x 40 cm (24 x 16 in). This intriguing mixed-media construction
explores the boundaries of three-dimensional structure and
pattern. The artist comments: 'Specifically with this work I was
interested in the associations we make with floral imagery, in
this case the use of the term "flower head". The work utilizes
heads of 20th Century leaders, which are placed at the centre
of each embroidered shape. The form of the work references
a pincushion set into a mirror, and at the end of each metal pin
is placed a portrait head. Leaders are very conscious of their
appearance, hence the reflectivity of the imagery and the oblique
understated duality of the term "pinhead".'
(Right) detail image

Katie Pasquini-Masopust 'Big Sticks' 152 x 178 cm (60 x 70 in).
This large quilt, which is packed full of snippets of differently
coloured, patterned and textured fabrics, was inspired by
a big pile of sticks that the artist walked by every morning.
She comments: 'I used bright colours for each stick with the
complementary colour for the shadows. Black and white were
added to represent the dead old sticks and the brilliant colours
are the promise of new growth.'

Elena Corchero 'Graphic Necklace' detail. Project sponsored by 'Distance Lab'; www.distancelab.org. Special thanks to Crispin Jones's collaboration for electronics; www.mr-jones. org. Electronic components, for example solar cells, resistors and LEDs, are integrated directly into the hand- and machine-embroidered lace in this textile necklace and are wired together into working circuits using conductive thread. This collection of solar powered items aims not to hide technology but to disguise it in a beautiful and stylistic way, making it appeal to a new clientele.

Donatella Crippa 'Centrepiece' 34 x 27 cm (13.5 x 10.5 in).
Redolent of Scandinavian folk art images, this image was inspired
by a 'Pennsylvania Dutch' design that the artist saw painted on a
trunk in a museum in Canada. She always looks for images that
tell a story, and the simplicity of the basket of flowers and fruits
spoke of care, kindness and times gone by. The artist continues:

'For this piece, I chose vintage fabrics mainly for their organic
qualities. The fabrics I thought were too "new looking" so I
brushed with a quite heavy coat of bleach to achieve a faded,
well-worn look. I then hand quilted the background with tiny little
stitches in rustic colours.'

Donatella Crippa 'I Wish I Had Giraffes' 39 x 26 cm (15 x 10.25 in). Created in response to a documentary on African wildlife, this charming stitched and reverse appliquéd textile uses a variety of materials, old and new, and methods that include staining fabric with tea.

Laura McCafferty 'Man with Dog' 82 x 74 cm (32 x 29 in).
It is possibly the way the owner of this dog is delicately averting
his gaze while the dog cocks his leg against the vintage fabric
lamp post that lends an air of verisimilitude to this screen-printed,
stitched and appliquéd piece. The artist comments: 'I drew this
man and his dog in Barcelona. It was around the time when I
was documenting universal culture – the acts that happen in all
areas of the world that we can all relate to.'

Clare Lane 'Public Art Commission for Blackburn NHS Trust' **Detail of 9-m (29.5-ft) long triptych.** This photograph shows the final stitching phase of this piece, which arose from the artist's residency in Blackburn in the North of England. The theme was to draw from the architectural heritage and topography of the area, and to create a piece that reflected the people of Blackburn and their perceptions of the place. She explains: 'To this end, work with the local community was essential to the gathering of information about the character of the area, and group discussions and photographic projects were undertaken with hospital staff, patients and local community groups.'

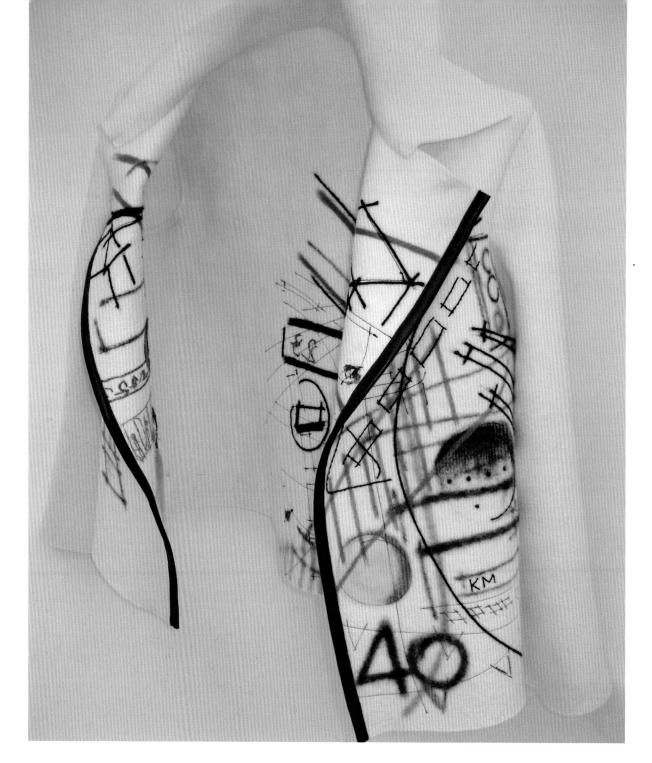

Emma Dillon 'Slade Lane' 65 x 55 cm (25.5 x 21.5 in). Covered in marks and part images of traffic signs and road markings, this hand felted women's wool jacket has been embellished and stitched. The artist comments: 'I am particularly interested in the idea of a recognizable motif or word amongst a collection of abstract marks. I find that handmade felt allows me to translate the qualities of my drawn marks most effectively. I also enjoy the density and relief effect created by stitch into felt, and work from the front and reverse of the fabric to create the different levels of marks.'

Katie Pasquini-Masopust 'Vivace' 124 x 122 cm (48.75 x 48 in).
Directly inspired by her abstract paintings, this artist interprets
and extends her work as stitched textiles. A small watercolour
was the catalyst for this piece. She explains: 'I then painted it in
acrylic pigment and the resulting painting was lacking, so I took it
outside and threw more paint on it. I could not make it any worse
but the thrown paint adds movement and depth. As a fibre piece,
I appliquéd colours to represent the thrown paint.'

Mai-Britt Axelsen (made in a workshop with Kate Cox) 'Bush Fire' 32 x 43 cm (12.5 x 17 in). This wall hanging was made by assembling loose layers of fibre and fabric and free-motion quilting them down onto a background.

Nadia Sparham 'Gold Tree Cushion' 40 x 40 cm (16 x 16 in).
The three-dimensionality of this tree shape has been achieved by
screen-printing with foiling, using a net curtain as a resist.
The unadorned trunk outline was created by appliqué and
machine embroidery.

Nadia Sparham 'Button Tree Brown Cushion' 40 x 40 cm (16 x
16 in). Labyrinthine stitching with buttons strategically stitched in
place give this cushion an unusual texture. It has been screen-
printed and was inspired by a car engine casing.

Els van Baarle 35 x 150 cm (13.75 x 59 in) each. Inspired by the remains of the ancient Roman city of Pompeii, these two silk-based wall hangings have been screen-printed, dyed using wax resist, hand embroidered and stitched.
(Right) detail image

Poppy Treffry 2.5 cm (1 in) diameter. These cute little badges
continue this artist's preoccupation with tea, cups and long
legged birds, and were inspired by the need to use up tiny scraps
of fabrics left over from making larger pieces.

Michael Brennand-Wood detail (top) 113 x 166 x 10 cm (44.5 x 65 x 4 in). This inventive and innovative multimedia construction draws on references from embroidery, lace and a range of contemporary and biomorphic historical sources. The artist comments: 'I really feel with these pieces that I'm trying to orchestrate a visual sound and produce work that, at a critical distance, fuses into a resonant, intensely colourful multidimensional, rhythmic structure.'

Nadia Sparham 'Orange Bird Cushion' (above left) 30 x 40 cm (12 x 16 in). Inspired by children's drawings, a curious little round orange bird flies straight towards us in this appliquéd and machine embroidered cushion.

Laura McCafferty 'Pete's Coffee Bar' 70 x 46 cm (27.5 x 18 in).
Set in Nottingham's Victoria Centre in England, this screen-
printed and appliquéd view of an open-fronted coffee bar is from
a collection completed for an exhibition at Nottingham Castle
Museum in July 2005. The artist explains: 'I loved these two
women chatting as I walked past one busy lunch time. I like the
1970s feel created by the use of a retro pillowcase fabric.'

Clare Lane 'Mooney and Sons' 93 x 71 cm (36.5 x 28 in).
Based on a combination of photographs and digitally-combined
drawings, blocks of colour were 'painted' on the computer
before the image was hand stitched. The completed montage
is printed onto a textile surface, which is itself a pliant material,
and counters the hard structure of an architectural edifice. The
final process of stitching texture and line back into the piece
brings out a three-dimensional quality, which is an echo of
its source. The artist explains: 'The final picture may present
familiar fragments to spark recognition but skew perception and
challenge the viewer to reconsider their surroundings.'

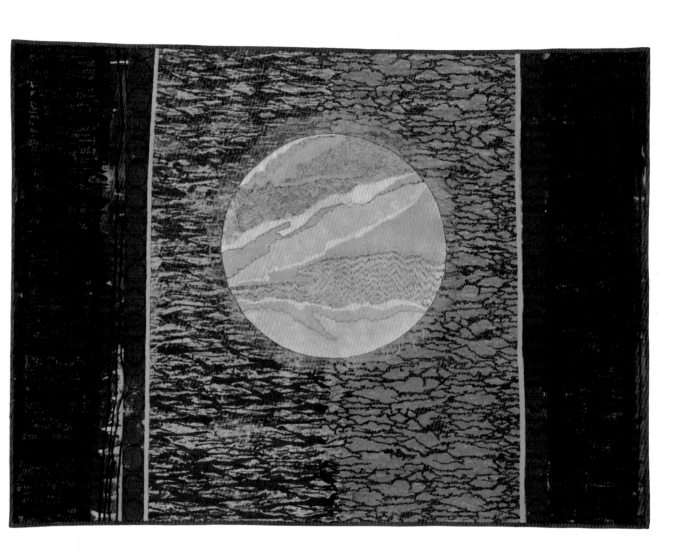

Jeanne Raffer Beck 'What Can't Be Stolen' 132 x 95 cm (52 x 37.5 in). This brightly-coloured painted and stitched textile piece has a poignant history. Stolen, unfinished, and later recovered by the police, the artist explains that by the time she completed the piece 'it had evolved into a personal declaration of overcoming; material things can be destroyed or stolen but our true treasures – our voice, our spirit, our creativity, our inner light – remain'.

Katie Pasquini-Masopust 'Leggiero' 203 x 203 cm (80 x 80 in).
Exploding colours resembling splashed bold brushstrokes have
been appliquéd onto a quilted background in this large piece. A
small portion of a larger acrylic painting created while listening
to music initially inspired this piece, and a line drawing was
subsequently created and enlarged to make the pattern.

Laura McCafferty 'Charlie and Heidi Buying Ice Cream' detail
65 x 56 cm (25.5 x 22 in). Affectionately observed, this printed
and appliquéd study of two friends buying ice cream from a van
is a charming study of ordinary life. The artist explains: 'With this
piece, I really wanted to begin to document the people close to
me rather than strangers who made me smile. I drew my two
friends Charlie and Heidi while on a day out in the Derbyshire
countryside. Everything was lovely that day, the bubble-shaped
ice cream van and their colourful outfits. It had to be pink and
girly. I used Heidi's granny's pyjamas for the sky.'

Jenni Cadman 'Passage' 63 x 90 cm (25 x 36 in). Vigorous lines have been created via free machine sewing and appliquéd around the central imagery, before being painted and distressed in this textile wall hanging inspired by Gulls Rock, Cornwall in England. The artist comments on her work: 'It has long been my quest to bring together the concepts of the painter with the craft skills of the stitcher and this is how I see myself... an artist who explores the painted or drawn mark through stitched textiles.'

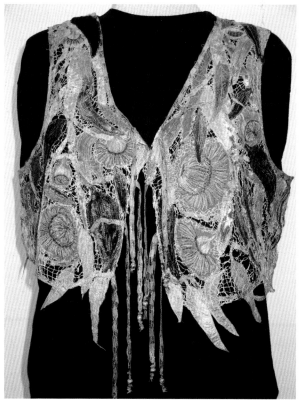

Kelly Woollard 'Mary' 65 x 49 cm (25.5 x 19 in). Reclaimed damask, calico and nylon sailcloth has been transformed through intricate, layered cutwork and embellishment techniques to create this one-off ornate fabric piece inspired by antique embroidery samplers.

Pamela Annesley 'Flowering Gum Waistcoat'. *Eucalyptus ficifolia* (the Australian flowering gum) inspired this delicately coloured waistcoat. The artist lives in a rural area north of Perth, western Australia, where there are many of these magnificent trees, known for producing coloured blossoms during the late summer months. She comments: 'I took photographs and made a small acrylic painting of the blossoms. I tried to emulate the blossoms in many shades of thread, made leaves from silk paper and added a ribbon to link all the features.'

Tait & Style 'Pom Bomb Pin Cushions' 20 cm (8 in) each in circumference. Pom Bomb pin cushions are an amusing and practical way to store pins and needles. The designers comment: 'This was designed by one of our workshop girls, Fiona Driver, as a pin cushion for herself. Ingrid liked them so much that she now sells them in our collection! They are made using 200 metres (650 feet) of 100% lambswool, which are dyed and then felted to make a smooth ball.'

Katie Pasquini-Masopust 'Tenemente' 157 x 124 cm (62 x 49 in).
Lines of splattered paint have been inferred by the sweeping
movements of the appliquéd fabric strips that criss-cross this
large quilt. 'Tenemente' is based on a section of one of the
artist's watercolour paintings.

Rosie Gregory 'Shelf' (top) 30 x 40 cm (12 x 15.75 in). Leather, wire and beaded flowers demonstrate a little of the wealth of variety present in nature. The forms of the flowers are greatly influenced by the materials that are used.

Laura McCafferty 'Lady with Tea' (above) 40 x 32 cm (16 x 12.5 in). A typical domestic scene of a woman drinking tea has been printed and appliquéd using vintage flower-patterned fabrics. The artist comments: 'This piece really captures my nana as she loves drinking tea and baking cake! I was quite interested in exploring domestic scenes around this time.'

Clare Lane 'City Scene' 115 x 85 cm (45 x 34 in). A building site in the city of London, with the dome of St Paul's cathedral just visible in the distance, is the subject of this digitally-printed and stitched canvas. The artist explains: 'My previous career in Surveying and Architecture forms the basis of a long-held fascination with our built habitat, and constantly informs what I do. Our urban environment is a dynamic, vibrant place in a constant state of flux and yet buildings are seen as static things – solid and immovable. This dichotomy fascinates me and now has me questioning how we see this environment, and the meanings we attribute to it.'

Kim Barnett for Birds in Skirts 'Tyvek handbag' (top)
15 x 15 cm (6 x 6 in). This experimental handbag is made from
Tyvek, the ubiquitous plastic, paper-like material often found in
packaging. The Tyvek has been screen-printed with a pattern of
knitting using puff binder.

Saskia Weishut-Snapper 'Creation of the World' (above)
108 x 82 cm (42.5 x 32 in). The intense colours used in these
mixed-media panels harmonize to produce a dramatic and
powerful piece that, for the artist, symbolizes creation.

Marie-Renée Otis 'La Tête Hors de L'eau' (The Head Out of Water) 36 x 30 cm (14 x 12 in). A cosmopolitan mix of resources has been incorporated into this mixed-media fantasy portrait, including: stranded cotton, silk, metallic thread, glass from India, glass from Nigeria, lapis lazuli, pearls, tubes, coral from the Bahamas, cowries from Central Africa, beads, snails from Cuba, shells and wool on canvas.

Kelly Woollard 'Constantine' 52 x 52 cm (20.5 x 20.5 in). Layered, painted and glued, this innovative multicoloured photo frame is made from reclaimed damask fabric cut into an intricate pattern reminiscent of ornate period furnishings.

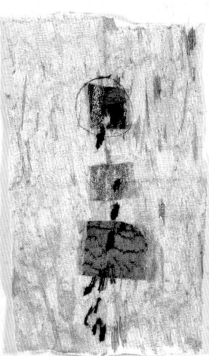

Alice Kettle 'In the Guise of an Angel' 90 x 40 cm (36 x 16 in)
each. This densely stitched machine embroidery is a triptych,
which incorporates patches of brilliant metallic colour like flashes
of a just-seen kingfisher, together with images of faces and
barely perceptible, not quite human forms.

Lorna Davis 23 x 32 cm (9 x 12.5 in). Cotton and silk fabrics have been bonded together and then discharge- and devoré-printed before being embroidered and stitched. The artist explains: 'I take pleasure in experimenting with processes and fabrics, to use them in a way that will alter the structure or appearance of the fabric.'

Elana Herzog Untitled piece from 'Civilizations and its Discontents' 100 x 50 cm (39.25 x 19.5 in). Combining pieces of Persian carpet together with other fabrics and staples on drywall panels, this artist has an unusual method of working. She explains: 'Found textiles are stapled to panels using thousands of metal staples. Parts of the fabric and the staples are then removed, leaving a residue of shredded fabric and perforated wall surface in some areas, and densely stapled and built-up areas elsewhere. The structure of the image is thus generated directly from the weave of the fabric.'

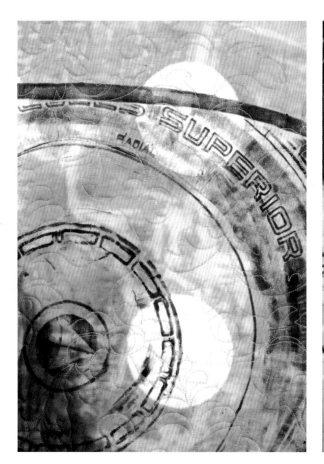

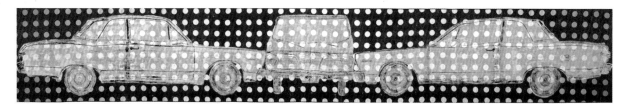

Bean Gilsdorf (above) 'Ghost' 1066 x 157 cm (420 x 62 in).
Commercially quilted, this dyed, painted and bleached textile is a
portrait of the artist's 1966 Plymouth Valiant car and took over a
year to create. The artist comments: 'At each step I was terrified
I was going to mess something up …13 continuous yards of
fabric is heartbreaking to ruin. I had to make myself work on it.
Now I can't wait to make another.'
(Top) close-up details

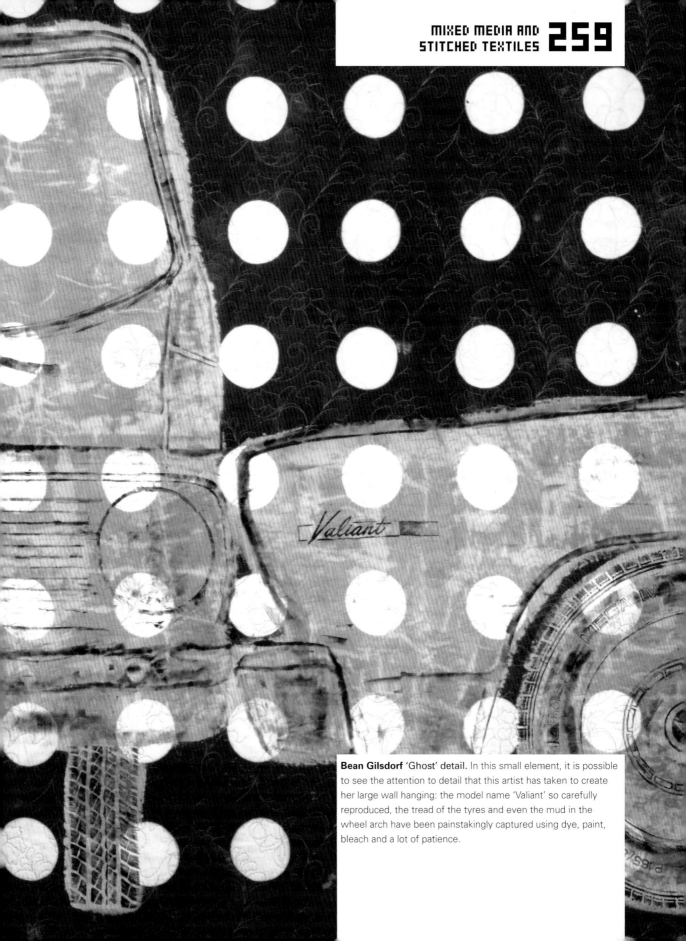

Bean Gilsdorf 'Ghost' detail. In this small element, it is possible to see the attention to detail that this artist has taken to create her large wall hanging: the model name 'Valiant' so carefully reproduced, the tread of the tyres and even the mud in the wheel arch have been painstakingly captured using dye, paint, bleach and a lot of patience.

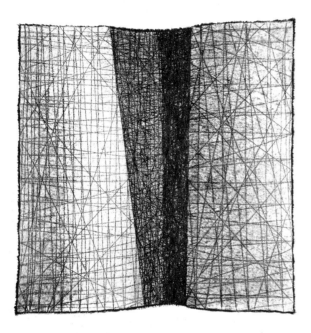

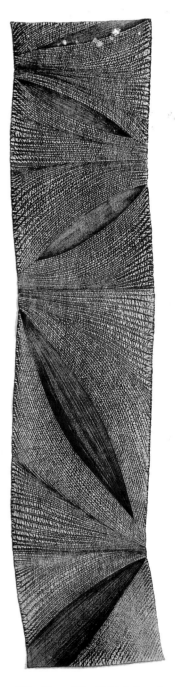

Diana Harrison 60 x 60 cm (24 x 24 in). Densely stitched, dyed, bleached and overprinted, this piece explores the tradition of quilting. The artist explains how its content can be traced to different sources, including travelling, the repetition of regular commuting, road-surface markings and curves, with lines crisscrossing, meshing and supporting. She continues: 'Together these remind one of the transience of life.'

Diana Harrison 250 x 52 cm (98 x 20.5 in). Focusing on the tactile and visual qualities that result from dyeing, layering, stitching and bleached overprinting of cloth, this piece combines the shrinking, stretching and subsequent distortion created through the process. The artist comments further: 'Traces of stitching are revealed through the discharging out of the dyed ground, so that the cloth and thread become one.'

Paddy Killer 'Researching Grandfather' 91 x 77 cm (36 x 30 in).
This artist has captured an extraordinarily detailed analysis of her
grandfather's life in drawing, painting and machine embroidery.
She used scanned and digital camera images, drawing with her
digital tablet and pen to make the piece look as if it is a document
on an old AppleMac display, with layers and menus and
windows. She explains: 'I printed it out and made many samplers
to decide on the colours and threads. Then I drew on the silk
with technical pens, painted and then machine embroidered it
using a darning foot and fine threads.'

Susan Taber Avila 'In my Closet' 31 x 40 cm (12.25 x 16 in) each panel. Evidently inspired by an obsessive need to organize her closet, these shoe pictures were digitally-printed onto cotton sateen and stitched onto layers of industrial felt and muslin remnants to form a quilt. The artist continues: 'After photographing all of my shoes I realized that they formed an image of my identity that wasn't what I expected – most of the shoes are low heeled, rubber soled, and most of all practical, not what I would imagine of a fashion design professor!' (Opposite) close-up detail

Lorna Davis 36 x 43 cm (14 x 17 in). Tough, durable Tyvek was heated to create a sculptural surface to this unusual hand dyed, printed and embroidered fabric sample. The artist explains: 'By using different methods of heating and different lengths of time I was able to see how the fabric could be sculptured and in turn create new and exciting surfaces.'

Susan Taber Avila 'Fragments' detail (see opposite)

Susan Taber Avila 'Fragments' 182 x 145 cm (71.5 x 57 in). Remnants of silk charmeuse were dyed, discharged and pieced into a base construction that floats over a layer of openwork stitching in this piece, which explores the subtleties of space and particles contained within the universe. The artist comments on her characteristic stitching technique: 'While stitching is often used for surface embellishment (embroidery) or joining materials, my work is unique in that I simultaneously develop both the structure and surface of an object through the stitching process.' She is committed to stitching constructions because this ubiquitous method, prevalent throughout history, still has something new to say, and stitching creates a mark, adds colour and defines the structure.

GLOSSARY

Arashi: pole-wrapped resist; fabric is wrapped diagonally around a cylindrical object, bound and tightly compressed before dyeing.

Batik: wax-resist dyeing; fabric is painted, sprayed or printed with molten wax, which forms a barrier to the dye.

Devoré: a chemical process whereby one type of fibre from a mixed-fibre woven fabric is dissolved, leaving a characteristic loss of pile in that area.

Deconstructed printing: also known as *breakdown* printing, this method involves applying dye paste to a screen, allowing it to dry, and then printing with sodium alginate onto the substrate beneath.

Discharge printing: a technique that uses a chemical paste to remove dye from selected areas.

Double weave: this weaving method utilizes two sets of warp and weft yarns, creating two separate layers of fabric that produce a design when both sets of yarn change position, interlocking the layers at that point.

Ecoprint: an ecologically sustainable, plant-based printing process that gives brilliant colour to cloth, originated by the artist India Flint.

Gutta or gutta-serti: a latex-rubber solution that creates a resist to the dye.

Ikat: an Indonesian term for the binding and resist dyeing of warp and weft threads before they are woven.

Illuminating dyes: colours that can be added in place of areas of dyes that are removed during the discharge process.

Indigo: the source of the colour blue and used as a dye for many millennia. It was finally synthesized in 1897.

Itajime shibori: clamp-resist dyeing.

Kasuri: a traditional Japanese hand dyed, hand woven fabric made with tied warp and weft threads using a technique similar to *ikat*.

Katazome: paste resist that is applied using a stencil.

Komasu shibori: a technique that produces small squares on the fabric.

Leheriya: a traditional resist technique originating in Rajasthan, India. The cloth is rolled diagonally, bound in selected areas and dyed, often repeatedly, to produce a design of complex diagonal lines.

Leno: a weaving technique whereby pairs of yarns are twisted between each weft insertion.

Natural indigo: found in the leaves of many different plants worldwide, including *Isatis tinctoria* (woad) in Europe and western Asia, and *Polygonum tinctorium* (dyer's knotweed) in China and Japan.

Noren: a traditional partition used in Japanese homes.

Rozome: the Japanese term for wax-resist dyeing.

Shibori: shaped-resist dyeing.

Sukumo: the traditional Japanese dyestuff produced from *Polygonum tinctorium* (dyer's knotweed). It is fermented in wood-ash lye to create a natural indigo vat.

CONTRIBUTORS

A
Helen Suzanne Alexander
helen@hebart.co.uk
www.hebart.co.uk

Pamela Annesley
info@textileworkshops.com
www.textileworkshops.com

Mai-Britt Axelsen
ma@closaucomte.com

B
Els van Baarle
elsvanbaarle@zeelandnet.nl
www.elsvanbaarle.com

Sandra Backlund
info@sandrabacklund.com
www.sandrabacklund.com

Kim Barnett
birds.in.skirts@googlemail.com
www.birds.in.skirts.com

Brian Barratt
brian.barratt1@ntlworld.com

Cressida Bell
cb@cressidabell.com
www.cressidabell.com

Laura Bissonnet
notnicelaura@hotmail.com
www.notnicelaura.co.uk

Jason Black
jblack@ntlworld.com

Rebecca Blackburn
becblack@fsmail.net

Helen Bolland
mail@helenbolland.co.uk
www.helenbolland.co.uk

Dorothy Bunny Bowen
bunny@db-bowen.com
www.db-bowen.com

Michael Brennand-Wood
michael@brennand-wood.com
www.brennand-wood.com

Sofie Brünner
brnner@yahoo.com

Mary-Clare Buckle
mary-clare.buckle@1-art-1.com
www.1-art-1.com

Danielle Budd
danielle@missbudd.com
www.missbudd.com

C
Walkiria Caramico
walkiria@walkiria.com.br
www.walkiria.com.br

Jenni Cadman
jennicadman@gmail.com
www.jennicadman.co.uk

Liz Clay
liz@lizclay.co.uk
www.lizclay.co.uk

Drusilla Cole
druvcole@aol.com
www.drusillacole.co.uk

Elena Corchero
elena@lostvalues.com
www.lostvaues.com

Donatella Crippa
doni@donifolk.com
www.donifolk.com

D
Arthur David
arthurdavid@arthurdavid.ch
www.arthurdavid.ch

Lorna Davis
lornadavis21@hotmail.com

Rose de Borman
rdeborman@gmail.com

Emma Dillon
emmadillon@mac.com
www.emmadillon.com

Yun Ding
dingyundeila@hotmail.com

F
Barbara Fidoe
bafidoe@yahoo.co.uk
www.axisweb.org/artist/
barbarafidoe

Deanne Fitzpatrick
info@hookingrugs.com
www.hookingrugs.com

India Flint
mail@indiaflint.com
www.indiaflint.com

G
Bean Gilsdorf
bean@beangilsdorf.com
www.beangilsdorf.com

Kerr Grabowski
kerr@kerrgrabowski.com
www.kerrgrabowski.com

Sally Greaves-Lord
sally.greaves-lord@virgin.net

Charlotte Grierson
weave@charlottegrierson.com
www.charlottegrierson.com

Rosie Gregory
rosie@rosiegregory.co.uk
www.rosiegregory.co.uk

Ulla Gustavsson for Virtuelli
Design Studio
ulla@virtuelli.se
www.virtuelli.se

H
Lara Hailey
larahailey@hotmail.com
www.larahailey.co.uk

Afet Halil
afet_halil@hotmail.com

Ehalill Halliste
ehalill.halliste@mail.ee
www.ehalillhalliste.com

Diana Harrison
dianaharrison@hotmail.co.uk

Elana Herzog
elana@elanaherzog.com
www.elanaherzog.com

Caitlin Hinshelwood
c.hinshelwood@yahoo.co.uk
www.caitlinhinshelwood.co.uk

Pat Hodson
pat@pathodson.co.uk
www.pathodson.co.uk

Kate Hyde
K8hyde@yahoo.com
www.katehyde.co.uk

I
Mie Iwatsubo
mietsubo@hotmail.com

K
Jane Keith
studio@janekeith.com
www.janekeith.com

Marianne Kemp
info@horsehairweaving.com
www.horsehairweaving.com

Alice Kettle
alice.m.kettle@bigfoot.com
www.alicekettle.com

Paddy Killer
paddy@paddykillerart.co.uk
www.paddykillerart.co.uk

Joanna Kinnersley-Taylor
joanna@joannakinnerslytaylor.
com
www.joannakinnerslytaylor.com

Angelika Klose
angeli.k@gmx.net
www.angeli-k-hutdesign.de

Anne Kyyrö Quinn
info@annekyyroquinn.com
www.annekyyroquinn.com

L
Clare Lane
clare@urban-fabric.co.uk
www.urban-fabric.co.uk

Sue Lawty
lawty@suelawty.co.uk
www.suelawty.co.uk

M
Laura Mackay
laura@mackay.fslife.co.uk

Satu Makkonen
for Hau Hauz
info@hauhauz.com
www.hauhauz.com

Ptolemy Mann
fifth@ptolemymann.com
www.ptolemymann.com

Prudence Mapstone
prudence@knotjustknitting.com
www.knotjustknitting.com

Natasha Marshall
info@natashamarshall.com
www.natashamarshall.com

Katherine Maxwell
katlmax@hotmail.com
www.katherinemaxwell.com

Laura McCafferty
laura@lauramcafferty.com
www.lauramcafferty.com

Hannah McMahon
for Zedzz.co.uk
sales@zedzz.co.uk
www.zedzz.co.uk

Latifa Medjdoub
info@latifamedjdoub.com
www.latifamedjdoub.com

Helen Melvin
helenmelvin@fieryfelts.co.uk
www.fieryfelts.co.uk

Alicia Merrett
alicia@tufpark.demon.co.uk
www.tufpark.demon.co.uk

Lidia Muro
lidiamuro44@hotmail.com

N
Carol Naylor
carol@carolnaylor.co.uk
www.carolnaylor.co.uk

Lene Nordfeldt Iversen
ln_i@webspeed.dk
www.lene-nordfeldt-iversen.dk

Nya Nordiska
secretary@nya.com
www.nya.com

O
Saori Okabe
saoriokabe@hotmail.com

Laura-Jane O'Kane
laura_okane@hotmail.co.uk

Marie-Renée Otis
marene@caramail.com

P
Panayiota Panayiotou
pennipanayiotou@yahoo.co.uk
www.bubble-tree.com/
pennipanayiotou

Deepa Panchamia
info@deepapanchamia.com
www.deepapanchamia.com

Robin Paris
robin@robinparis.co.uk
www.robinparis.co.uk

Jeung-Hwa Park
jeunghwa.park@gmail.com

Katie Pasquini-Masopust
katiepm@aol.com
www.katiepm.com

Sarah Pearson Cooke
sarah@sarahpearsoncooke.com
www.sarahpearsoncooke.com

Marion Piffaut
piffautmarion@yahoo.fr
www.marionpiffaut.com

Jessica Preston
jesspreston43@hotmail.com
www.jessicapreston.com

R
Jeanne Raffer Beck
beckwriter@aol.com
www.jeannebeck.com

Naomi Renouf
textileart@naomirenouf.co.uk
www.naomirenouf.co.uk

Chinami Ricketts
chinami@rickettsindigo.com
www.rickettsindigo.com

Rowland Ricketts III
rowland@rickettsindigo.com
www.rickettsindigo.com

Luanne Rimel
lrimel@mindspring.com

S
Ismini Samanidou
ismini@isminisamanidou.com
www.isminisamanidou.com

Joan Schulze
joan@joan-of-arts.com
www.joan-of-arts.com

Tilleke Schwarz
info@tillekeschwarz.com
www.tillekeschwarz.com

Margo Selby
margo@margoselby.com
www.margoselby.com

Zakee Shariff
contact@zakeeshariff.com
www.zakeeshariff.com

Suzanne Silk
silk@suzannesilk.com
www.suzannesilk.com

Ingrid Sixsmith
ingrid@ingridsixsmith.com
www.ingridsixsmith.com

Arlé Sklar-Weinstein
arlesklar@yahoo.com
www.arlesklar.com

Mandy Southan
southan.mandy@virgin.net

Nadia Sparham
nadia@nadiasparham.co.uk
www.nadiasparham.co.uk

Betsy Sterling Benjamin
betsy@bsb.com
www.betsysterlingbenjamin.
com

Karen Stiehl Osborn
karen@karenstiehlosborn.com
www.karenstiehlosborn.com

Christina Strutt
for Cabbages and Roses
amyg@cabbagesandroses.com
www.cabbagesandroses.com

Sari Syväluoma
info@syvaluoma.com
www.syvaluoma.com

T
Susan Taber Avila
susan@suta.com
www.suta.com

Ingrid Tait
for Tait & Style.co.uk
info@taitandstyle.co.uk
www.taitandstyle.co.uk

Tiziana Tateo
vtateo@alice.it
www.tizianatateo.it

Laura Thomas
info@laurathomas.co.uk
www.laurathomas.co.uk

Sharon Ting
sbting@aol.com

Ilkka Timonen
for Virtuelli Design Studio
ilkka@timonen.se
www.virtuelli.se

Timorous Beasties
info@timorousbeasties.com
www.timorousbeasties.com

Poppy Treffry
hello@poppytreffry.co.uk
www.poppytreffry.co.uk

Melin Tregwynt
design@melintregwynt.co.uk
www.melintregwynt.co.uk

W
Carole Waller
carole@carolewaller.co.uk
www.carolewaller.co.uk

Saskia Weishut-Snapper
saskia@weishut.com
www.saskia.weishut.com

Christine White
chrisawhite@charter.net
www.chrisawhite.com

Isabella Whitworth
mail@isabellawhitworth.co.uk
www.isabellawhitworth.co.uk

Laura Willits
laurawillits@laurawillits.com
www.laurawillits.com

Alison Willoughby
alison@alisonwilloughby.com
www.alisonwilloughby.com

Marie Wright
marie.wright@ukgateway.net
www.marie-wright.co.uk

Lois Woodger
loisw@waitrose.com
www.loiswoodger.co.uk

Kelly Woollard
kelwoollard@hotmail.com
www.kelouisedesigns.co.uk

Y
Dionne Yang
dionne.yang@gmail.com

Yu Chu Amanda Yuen
amandadayuen@gmail.com

Charlotte Yde
charlotte@yde.de
www.yde.dk/charlotte

PHOTO CREDITS

The author and publisher would like to thank the following institutions and individuals for providing photographic images for use in this book. In all cases, every effort has been made to credit the copyright holders, but should there be any omissions or errors the publisher would be pleased to insert the appropriate acknowledgement in any subsequent edition of this book.

Where no credit is listed here it should be assumed that the artists have photographed their own work.

10 John Polak Photography
15 (left) Rowland Ricketts III
16 Kathryn E Martin and Christine Downes
17 Andrew Green
18 Rowland Ricketts III
19 Indrek Juhani
20 Rogier Chang
22 (left) Kathryn E Martin and Christine Downes
22 (right) Sing Lo
23 (bottom) Iain Davies
25 Karen Philippi
26 Denise Grünstein
27 (top) Iain Davies
28 (right) John Polak Photography
28 (left) Karen Philippi
30 Karen Philippi
32 Naoto Okamoto
37 (left) Karen Philippi
43 Sing Lo
44 Frank Thurston
45 (left) Rowland Ricketts III
46 Sing Lo
47 (right) Karen Philippi
48 Andrew Green
49 (bottom) Rogier Chang
50 Karen Philippi
52 Dimity Mapstone
55 Mark Llewellyn
61 Andrew Green
63 Dimity Mapstone
65 John Polak Photography
68 (top) John Polak Photography
69 Calle Stoltz
71 (left) Peter Kelleher, courtesty of V&A images
71 (right) Jimmy McClean
72 Sing Lo
73 (left) Oscar Falk
73 (right) Jeffery James
73 Jeffrey James
74 (top) Jerry Hardman-Jones
75 Tass Kyprianou
76 Matt Jessop

78 John Polak Photography
80 (right) Kim Barr
83 Rogier Chang
86 Birthe Haumoller
88 Mike Hodson
99 (bottom) Stina Glommi
106 (bottom) right Noah Chen
107 Simon Ranshaw
120 Paul Glickman
121 Joop van Houdt
125 Mark Burden
126 (bottom) Andrew Wares
130 fpvc.com
135 Joop van Houdt
136 Angela Kidner
145 (left) fpvc.com
146 Simon Ranshaw
147 Simon Ranshaw
148 David Ellis
148 (right) Martin Phillimore
150 Ruth Clark
160 (bottom) Stina Glommi
166 Ruth Clark
170 (right) M Fernald
173 (bottom) Andrew Wares
175 (right) Martin Phillimore
176 (right) Paul Glickman
177 (right) Ursula Steiger
178 (left) fpvc.com
184 G Samson
187 Matthew Graham
193 (right) Helen Suzanne Alexander-Hebart
202 Lee Fatherree
203 Tas Kyrianou
205 Lee Fatherree
222 Andrew Gillis
224 Niels Jensen
235 Carolyn Wright
238 Joop van Houdt
244 Andrew Gillis
253 David Ellis
254 (left) Yves Tessier
257 Hermann Feldhaus
260 David Westwood
262 Lee Fatherree
265 Philip Cohen

BIBLIOGRAPHY

Atkins, Jacqueline M. (Ed). *Wearing Propaganda: Textiles on the Home Front*. Yale Press: BGC 2005

Balfour-Paul, Jenny. *Indigo*. London: British Museum Press 1998; Archetype Publications Ltd., 2006

Benjamin, Betsy Sterling. *The World of Rozome: Wax-Resist Textiles of Japan*. Reprint 2002. Tokyo: Kodansha International, 1996

Brito, Karen. *Shibori*. New York: Watson Guptill Publications 2002

Cardon, Dominique, *Natural Dyes, Sources, Tradition, Technology and Science*. Paris: Éditions Belin 2003, Archetype Publications Ltd., 2007

Cole, Drusilla. *Patterns – New Surface Design*. London: Laurence King Publishers 2007

Cole, Drusilla. *1000 Patterns*. London: A & C Black 2003

Dale, Julie. *Art-to-Wear*. New York: Abbeville Press 1986

Fogg, Marnie. *Couture Interiors*. London: Laurence King Publishers 2007

Ghisotti, Andea and Carletti Alessandro. *Red Sea Diving Guide*. Shrewsbury: Swan Hill Press 1997

Jackson, Lesley. *Robin & Lucienne Day*. London: Mitchell Beazley 2001

Nakano, Eisha and Stephan Barbara B., *Japanese Stencil Dyeing*. Tokyo: John Weatherhill 1982

Rayner, Geoffrey et al. *Artists' Textiles in Britain 1945-70*. London: Antique Collectors' Club.

Völker, Angela. *Textiles of the Weiner Werkstätte*. London: Thames and Hudson 1994

Wada, Yoshiko Iwamoto. *Memory on Cloth:* Tokyo. Kodansha International. 2002

Wada, Yoshiko Iwamoto, Mary Kellogg Rice and Jane Barton. *Shibori: The Inventive Art of Japanese Shaped-Resist Dyeing*. Reprint 1999: Tokyo. Kodansha International 1983